The Bottom Line

A Book of Business Ballads

The Bottom Line

A Book of Business Ballads

Bertie Ramsbottom

Century Publishing
London

First published in Great Britain in 1985
by Century Hutchinson Ltd
Brookmount House
62–65 Chandos Place, London WC2N 4NW

British Library Cataloguing in Publication Data

Windle, Ralph
    The bottom line : business ballads.
    I. Title
    821'.914   PR6068.A/

ISBN 0–7126–1057–X

Photoset by Deltatype, Ellesmere Port

Printed in Great Britain in 1985 by
Butler & Tanner Ltd, Frome, Somerset

Also available from Century:

Forked Tongues	Graham Jones
Own Goals	Graham Jones
Terse Verse	Cyril Fletcher
Way of the Wally	Kevin W Parsons

Acknowledgements

To generations of poets, beyond my emulation, who left their rhythms, rhymes, meters and alliterations buzzing in my head, and mangled in my verses – perhaps especially Housman, Eliot, Wordsworth and Betjeman.

To Gene Knight, who first taught me about the magic of words and books.

To Sir Peter Parker, for encouraging me from the start in my odd mode of communication, and showing how to be literate and civilised is not incompatible with business success.

To countless colleagues, friends, students and acquaintances in the business and academic world for supplying my material and responding to it with good humour – recognising, I hope, that my satire is a form of flattery and sign of affection.

To Ariana

- whose images of ewes and lambs,
first switched him on to dithyrambs;
and then, in honour of their sire,
named Bertie, *Rams*bottom, Esquire.

A CORPORATE PRAYER

Bless us Lord, and help us live,
Like every good executive,
A life more selflessly inclined
To what is in our Owner's mind;
And may it be Thy wish, and his,
To tell us what his thinking is,
The way it was when we began,
Before we had the Corporate Plan.

Help Thy servants on the Board
Understand his words, O Lord,
Since he changed his erstwhile manners,
And joined the Long Range Corporate Planners;
And if he needs must bore the pants off
All of us with Igor Ansoff,
Help us understand the charts —
Even the Synergetic parts.

Help us share his new perspectives,
That Strategies are not Objectives;
And, through Thy goodness, cross the ditch
To know more clearly which is which;
And, by Thy mercy which begat us,
Show us why it really matters,
In the name of Him who knows
All about Scenarios.

Grant us, Father, if you please,
Purer methodologies;
And tempt us not towards decisions
Without a further few revisions,
At interminable lengths,
Of our Weaknesses and Strengths.
Let need for action not deflect us
From codifying all our Vectors.

Grant, in answer to our prayers,
Thicker Strategies than theirs,
Who, in their blind unwisdom, chase
Profits in the market place,
Without a contemplative look
At what is in the Corporate Book.
Let their successes not distract us
From listing our External Factors.

Help us keep our Corporate eyes on
Some appropriate horizon,
Far from all the symptomatic
Signs of anything pragmatic;
Defend us, always, through our prayers,
From acting like entrepreneurs,
And from the uninformed who said
That, in the longer-term we're dead.

Contents

The Ultimate Guide to the Organisation

MARKETING AND SALES

PERSONNEL AND ORGANISATION

THE STAKE HOLDERS

The Best of
Boardroom Ballads

More Verses on the Office Wall

Contents

Dear Reader,

Bertie Ramsbottom does not suggest that the Business Life is an endless orgy of rollicking fun. Heading for the door with your latest dismissal notice can seem quite a bruising experience at the time.

Nevertheless, if you add to its more obvious laughs the unconscious humour of the corporate existence, something a good deal less tormented than the murderous mayhem suggested by the business commentators seems to emerge. A sensitive soul, and even good-will, often lurks behind the grim exterior of the thrusting, aggressive business executive. Even Chairmen and Presidents of World Corporations still belong to the human race, and can be looked on with a more loving eye which sees the timid child behind the towering achiever, and the fond uncle behind the Corporate Scrooge.

The great humanizer is the smile, and the gentle reminder that Business, too, is played out in that Great Theatre of the Absurd, which constitutes human life. Only thus are we reminded that we are all very minor gods in the vast order of the Universe, and brought to take a more benign view of each other's oddities and pretensions.

Like Caesor's Gaul, this Bertie Ramsbottom collection is divided into Three Parts.
Part One is to help you find your personal space in the Organisation, and where you fit, or aspire to fit, in the Great Business Scheme of Things. Secure in this knowledge,
Part Two re-assembles what seem to have been the favourites in his Boardroom Ballads, wherein the great phenomena of Business — such as the Multinational Corporation, the ubiquitous Business Consultant, and the proper mode of Corporate Prayer — are, at last, totally explained. And Part Three, a predominantly cheerful celebration of the indomitable spirit of the Business Professional against all odds, should leave you singing on your way, up or down the Corporate snakes and ladders.

For Bertie Ramsbottom, he (or she) is most blessed who travels hopefully even if he fails to arrive! As we slither around on the lower, or middle, slopes of the corporate Himalayas, we need spoil none of the exhilaration of the climb by envying those already on the summit. They, we know, have nowhere else to go but down!

Sincerely!

Ralph Windle

The Ultimate Guide to the Organisation

The Board

THE DIRECTORS

Directors are the firm's élite;
They fall, but mainly on their feet;
For once they have their Board regalia
Most seem impervious to failure;
And changes, when the critics frown,
Are mainly somewhat lower down.

They come in two quite separate blends,
Professionals, and Chairman's friends;
The former tested by survival,
The latter non-executival;
The first have offices and functions,
The second don't, except for luncheons.

We love our Board, and hold them dear,
So long as they don't interfere.

THE CHAIRMAN

A Chairman is the link between
A business, and its bigger scene.
That's why we choose from Knights and Lords,
Field Marshalls who have sheathed their swords,
Or other charismatic bosses,
To be our corporate Colossus.

He takes our ritualistic beating
At the Annual General Meeting;
But, that apart, his duty lies
In floating grandly in the skies,
Until some merger, bid or mess
Requires that he address the press.

'Distance lends enchantment' lies
Beneath what Chairmen symbolise.

THE MANAGING DIRECTOR

Managing Directors
Take decisions which affect us;
For, while other Board Room voices
Argue departmental choices,
In the end they all agree —
Where the buck stops, there sits he!

The vortex, where his life is lived, is
The corporate Scylla and Charybdis;
With, watching every course he steers,
Both shareholders and mutineers,
And bankers bobbing here and there
Seeking signs of mal de mer.

They love him, if he makes the trip;
If not, he goes down with the ship.

19

THE FINANCE DIRECTOR

Finance is the solar plexus,
Where most the foot of Fate affects us;
So he who understands the money,
Rules the hive and gets the honey.
Finance rules, by sacred lore,
With its Directors, things of awe!

As keepers of the Sacred Flame,
And business gods, in all but name,
They shroud the others' plans within
Forebodings of despair and sin;
Denounce the wicked risk or loan,
As if the money were their own.

They purify our pagan ranks,
Then seek redemption in the banks.

THE SALES DIRECTOR

Sales Directors are the stars
Who lead the corporate hussars;
For, not withstanding product science,
Nothing's won until the clients,
Terrorised by his marauders,
Capitulate and place the orders.

So, in the Boardroom mess, they wear
A soupçon of the debonnair;
Though some are still around, we find,
Who lead their armies from behind.

The gods of War, they know, are fickle,
And he who loses gets the sickle;
But while they're winning, joy prevails
Around our Cavaliers of Sales.

THE MARKETING DIRECTOR

A Marketing Director's years
Are somewhat younger than his peers;
He bombs the Board with new ideas.

The Chairman treats him like a son,
But when he speaks, the others run,
Or tell him why it can't be done.

If the oyster needs the grit
To form the pearl, then he is it!
Abrasion is his requisite.

They tolerate his youthful zest,
Assume he'll grow up like the rest,
And learn the quiet life's the best.

Let's hope they're wrong, one way or other;
Or, if they're right, they'll find another!

THE PRODUCTION DIRECTOR

A Board is a Board, in the eyes of the Lord,
And directors are equals and brothers;
But it's equally true, there are maybe a few
Who are not quite as equal as others!

It's a question of code, and of what's à-la-mode,
And the nuance of social decisions,
Which puts Finance and Sales on equivalent scales,
But Production in lower divisions.

For to make or produce was the prince of taboos,
In the days of the gentleman trader,
While the Board was a club, where a feller should snub
Such a crude, dirty-handed invader!

The Production Director, since washing his fingers,
Is allowed above-stairs — but the memory lingers!

THE PERSONNEL DIRECTOR

In the Boardroom, somewhat lonely,
While the others hah and hoo,
Sits a silent figure only
Speaking when (s)he's spoken to;
In among the caterwauling —
Markets, profits, what to sell —
Comes a still, small voice recalling
That the people count as well.
Everyone agrees they're for it,
Before proceeding to ignore it.

But Personnel Directors tend,
Within the Boardroom's changing facets,
To get the others in the end
To see that people *are* their assets.

23

Finance and Administration

THE CORPORATE PLANNERS

The view that Manners Makyth Man
Is de rigueur for those who plan;
The Future is a wanton japer,
Until they've captured it on paper;
But, safe in the Strategic Book,
It's tamed, and cannot run amuck.

Their strange, apocalyptic visions,
Shroud our corporate decisions,
In mists of mystical assumption,
Long on data, short on gumption!

'The Plan' may be an indoor sport,
Where Futurologists cavort;
Or Happiness, when Corporate Planners
Perceive it's *Man* that Makyth Manners.

THE ACCOUNTANTS

Accountants are a race apart,
Among the social-swingers,
For only they have made an Art
From counting on their fingers!

Their tools of trade to get ahead
Are pens and calculators,
With ink — some black, but mainly red —
And Institutes for status.

By looking, as the artist looks,
At debt, or tax affliction,
They've made the keeping of the Books
The highest form of fiction.

The rest may make and sell, but they
Most often have the final say!

THE AUDITORS

Auditors are mild and cautious,
Inoffensive and austere;
Mention of them turns men nauseous,
Furtive and inclined to fear;
Tends to blight their whole career.

It's the name that does the dirty;
'Auditor' means 'one who hears',
Not some over-bearing, shirty
Predator who interferes;
All an error, it appears!

Pusillanimously fussy,
Underneath he's just a pussy;
Smile at him, and stroke his fur —
He'll just roll on his back, and purr!

THE ESTIMATORS

To estimate, by definition,
Means guess, without too much precision;
So Estimators, one surmises,
Make guestimates for enterprises.
Let's hope the nonsense is the name,
And not the essence of the game!

In fact, they're men of mystic arts,
Who see the end before it starts;
The cost of projects, bits and pieces,
From first conception till it ceases.
They build their complex mental models
For fixing prices, in their noddles.
But others also count the cost,
When he who estimates is lost!

THE COMPANY SECRETARY

A Company Secretary
Is a self-effacing man;
Taciturn and unobtrusive,
So you catch him if you can!
But his ears are ever active,
And his eyes are everywhere;
And if something's for the record,
Like MacAvity, he's there!

He isn't quite a lawyer,
And he isn't quite a boss;
But he always has the answer,
And he's never at a loss!

Who was for it or agin, it's
Always somewhere in his minutes!

THE COMPANY LAWYERS

Legal men in corporations,
Thrive on doubts and hesitations;
Answer questions with another,
And 'on the one hand, on the other';
The art of sitting on the fence
Was built on legal precedents.

Their major task, beyond a doubt,
Is bailing the directors out;
When, in despair at 'pro' and 'anti',
They act, and find they're 'in flagrante'.
The lawyer's, meanwhile, with his claret,
Inside Regina versus Garrett!

The law's an ass? not so the classes,
Who clean up nicely as it passes!

THE COMPUTER MANAGER

Our revenue line is in heavy decline,
And the reasons are up for disputing;
But I go with the view which attributes it to
A malignant attack of computing.

In the days of our growth, we were too busy both
With our sales, and producing the latter,
To be able to play, as we have to today,
On our mounds of computerised data.

We've a manager, too, who has nothing to do
But to keep our Leviathan churning;
With an army on-line for its systems design,
And to soothe its statistical yearning.

Oh for the days when we'd only to grapple
With growing the business instead of the Apple!

THE CORPORATE ECONOMIST

Economists, like those at law,
Are masters of the 'either-or';
They speak, in dark and Delphic prose,
Of putative scenarios,
But will not be specific on
The Future, till it's been and gone;
And even then, they disagree
On how it was, or came to be!

They flatter our directors' brains
With supper-talk of Marx or Keynes,
But leave them feeling what's so wrong
With just plain muddling-along?

Thus Economics re-implants
The art of flying by your pants!

General
Manage-
ment
and
Produc-
tion

THE FACTORY MANAGER

Our Factory Manager contrives
A foot in two diverging lives;
Executive, behind his door,
And Charlie, on the factory floor.

So he, alone, is of the few
Who read the Times and Mirror, too;
And leap, as changing duty calls,
From pin-stripes into overalls.

Both workers and the staff extol
His twin-performance, on the whole;
But both connive with one another
To link him mainly with the other.
And yet his strength is not to be
The Devil *or* the Deep Blue Sea!

THE GENERAL MANAGERS

It would seem successful climbers up the business hierarchy are
Promoted to presiding over nothing in particular;
   It's much more honorific to abandon the specific,
And to *Generally* Manage, with a company car!

To become the perfect model of the modern General Manager,
You cultivate a distant, more abstracted, other-wordly air;
   But to Mary, Dick and Harry, you're an overhead to carry,
As you wait apotheosis to the Boardroom Chair!

To be properly promoted it's appropriate that you should be,
Apprised of all the pros and cons, and perquisites of strategy;
   You'll never make director, if the gods above detect a,
Predilection for the present actuality!

For it's only those of officer material and tenor'll
Be ultimately suitable for Managing-in-General.

THE PRODUCTION SCHEDULERS

Production Scheduling occasions
Fluctuating permutations,
Marked by moments of euphoria,
And frequent trips to sanitoria.

Forecasts flow in, hell for leather,
Variable as the weather,
Somewhere in the No-Mans-Land
Between the actual and planned;
And slithering about the slopes,
Between reality and hopes!

Perhaps the truth is not defiled
By paraphrasing Oscar Wilde —
Scheduling's the just conceivable
Pursuing the unbelievable!

RESEARCH AND DEVELOPMENT

*General
Manage-
ment
and
Produc-
tion*

To say what R and D men do
Infringes company taboo;
Security must never lapse
About what's underneath the wraps,
Until the final tests are clear —
Which always means another year!

Internally, the group comprises
Those in line for Nobel Prizes;
And a lesser group who lurk
Around to make the damn thing work.
The former sit, and think, and stammer;
The latter stand with wrench and hammer.

Both go wobbly at the knees,
At mention of the Japanese.

THE ENGINEERS

One thing of which we're never short
Is words — or so you might have thought;
But when it comes to 'engineers',
You'd think they're diamonds from De Beers!
We've spread the word around so thin,
There's little left that's not within.

If all were Earls who carried swords,
We'd all be in the House of Lords;
So why should all who own a spanner
Besport the Engineering banner?

It's time to put the word to bed,
Or find another term instead,
At least for those not yet aware
Brunel was *not* a Teddy Bear!

THE WORK STUDY TEAM

Work Study's at the equinox
And poised, with watches and with clocks,
To change the title of its church
To Operational Research;
But still committed by devotion
To principles of Time and Motion.

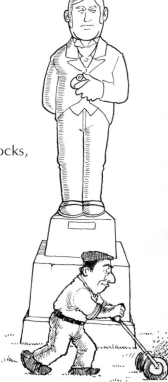

Anything that works or moves
Their transcendental skill improves;
Man, machine, renumeration
In perfect peace and calibration!
Inmune to heresy, and cries
That when they cure, the patient dies.

They stand, immortalised in rhyme —
'We also serve, who watch and time!'

THE CANTEEN MANAGER

*General
Manage-
ment
and
Produc-
tion*

Directors, strategies and such
May be essential to the plan,
But business life depends as much
On nourishing the inner-man.
What generals are prone to tell is
Truer of the corporate scenes;
These armies march upon their bellies,
Luncheon vouchers and canteens!

Canteen Managers and Chairmen
May inhabit different earths,
But the steak-and-kidney-pie-men
Have their own respective worths.

It's fish-and-chips and Irish Stews,
Which motivate the revenues!

33

THE FOREMEN AND THE SUPERVISORS

'Manager' is not a style
Much open to the rank and file;
But those a cut above the others
May join a lesser breed of brothers,
As Foremen and as Supervisors —
The N.C.O.s of enterprises.

The Supervisor's spurs are won
By knowing how the job is done,
Which tends to render him unique
Among the ruling corporate clique;
Who, though effusive with their thanks,
Prefer him in the 'other ranks'.

For Supervisors, by their natures,
Are still inclined to drop their aitches!

THE QUALITY CONTROLLERS

Quality Controllers
Are a race who grind their molars,
If each widget, quid and pro
Is not exactly 'comme-il-faut'.
Inoffensive with their mothers,
When at work they're something other,
With an eye invoking terror
For the qualitative error.

In pursuit of pure perfection,
They set standards for rejection
Which, with sensors, sums and samples,
Pose impossible examples.

Though we're not exactly for 'em,
All the customers adore 'em!

THE BUYERS

The back-legs in the panto-horse,
Evoke but little praise, of course;
And out-of-sight means out-of-mind
For those who man the firm's behind;
But Buyers are the motive force
Which drives the rear end of this horse!

Without their purchasing persistence,
No business-nag would make the distance;
They roam the world in planes and boats,
To bring the hungry beast its oats,
And all the bric-à-brac of life
That keep it from the knacker's knife.

Yet when it wins, by just a head, it
Often bites the hand that fed it!

Marketing and Sales

THE PRODUCT MANAGERS

Product Men are quick and pert,
(Like Brand Men, in some other places),
Elegant of suit and shirt,
And youngish, with cherubic faces!
What they do is — one supposes —
Rush around with files and charts,
Pushing keen, intrusive noses
Into all the working parts.

No one in the other sectors,
Seems to mind them, on the whole,
Playing managing directors,
Since there's little they control.

The mystery of last resort is
Where they go before their forties!

THE NEW PRODUCTS MAN

Our New Products man
Does the best that he can,
Like the eunuchs of old back in Persia;
But he feels like a lone
Sisyphus with his stone
On the slopes of our massive inertia.
And his product ideas
Propagate in his peers
A persistence in taking the Michael,
Since the one that we tried
Simply hiccupped and died
In the dawn of its product life-cycle.

But we like him around as the corporate kernel
Of our company motto that 'Hope Springs Eternal'.

THE PUBLIC RELATIONS TEAM

Public Relations people live
To emphasise the positive,
And wrap the world in glowing mentions
Of sympathy for our intentions.

But, lamentably, clients give
More focus on the negative,
And keep our P.R. people straining
With idiots who keep complaining.

To be both suitably evasive,
Yet always calm and non-abrasive,
Suggests a character between
A bishop and a schizophrene.

One only knows that they've succeeded,
At times when no-one thinks they're needed.

THE ADVERTISING TEAM

Advertising Men exude
A touch of class among the crude;
A small oasis, set apart,
Of creativity and art.

Their bold, imaginative vision
Of going big on television,
Stalls upon the never-ending
Tendency to prune their spending.
All their Oscar-winning subtle
Images invite rebuttal
From pedants much inclined to snigger
'Just make the bloody brand name bigger!'

That's why they sublimate their whims
With novels under pseudonyms.

THE MARKET RESEARCHERS

Our marketing researcher's nimble
Way with figures forms the symbol
Of our management's reliance
On exactitude and science.

Samples, studies and statistics,
From our anaylsts and mystics,
Form the data bases for
Our main decisions to ignore —
Except where what emerges, misses
Conflict with our prejudices.

Still, they cling to their elations
From their standard deviations,
While they learn research is part
Less of Science, than of Art!

THE DISTRIBUTION DEPARTMENT

Distribution and logistics
Is, to business pugilistics,
As provocative a pull
As the red rag to the bull!

All their optimal equations
For the products' destinations,
Topple over the escarpments
Pushed by all the main departments.

First, the salesmen want it hither,
Then production want it thither;
While the clients make suggestions
Not amenable to questions!

Of course, when everyone's in stock,
They'll say their budget's all to cock!

THE SALESMEN

Salesmen, of whatever races,
Look the same at fifty paces;
Notwithstanding girth or size,
Something lurking in their eyes
Indisputably asserts —
This guy's in Sales, so watch your shirts!

Salesmen must, however fearful,
Act indomitably cheerful,
Riding round their carousel
Of never-ending need to sell;
And knowing, if they meet their quota,
It's up, for each successive rota.

How they do it, no-one's saying;
But when they don't, it's time for praying.

40

THE EXPORT MANAGER

Export managers are known
For sitting by the linguaphone,
Perfecting, as we others can't
Their 'dans le jardin de ma tante',
And other abstruse words they utter
For gins and tonics in Calcutta.

Their office, though they're rarely there,
Has Gauloise fragrance in the air,
And other half-suggestive traces
Of journeys in romantic places.

To go with hope, but not arrive,
Is not how export men survive;
It's exile, once they've crossed the border,
And no way home without an order!

INDUSTRIAL RELATIONS

The I.R. man inclines to fuss
At phrases such as 'them' and 'us',
And tries to bridge the great divide,
Between the views of either side.

He pines for answers to the riddle
Of arbitrating from the middle.
Producing not just two, but three,
To reconcile — 'them', 'us' and 'he';
While both the others form a shared
Antipathy towards the third.

All the portents seem to presage
Pain for those who bring the message;
Yet like the rose they greet their dawns
To bloom, unloved, between the thorns.

THE RECRUITERS

Finding people who may suit us
Falls to corporate recruiters,
Expert in the art of seeing
The essence of a human being.

Extroverted in demeanour,
None exemplifies a keener
Nose for candidates who will
Incline to fingers in the till;
Or diagnose, in acned faces,
Propensities for going places.

Professional success consists
Of minds like psychoanalysts
And constitutions which enthuse
At à la carte with interviews.

EDUCATION AND TRAINING

Trainers are a strange assorted
Mix of teachers who aborted,
And executives with yearning
For the higher realms of learning.

To these dedicated creatures,
'He who cannot *do* it, teaches'
Is the not infrequent slur
At which to smile, but then demur;
For those who tend to say so neither
Do, nor try to teach it either!

And if we gave them, for their courses,
What we spend on training horses,
Maybe we would find it in us
To saddle more commercial winners!

THE PERSONNEL MANAGERS

Personnel, at best, supplies
The human face to enterprise,
Epitomising what it means
To say that men are not machines.

But Business is inclined to treasure
Mainly what accountants measure;
While Personnel performs its feats
Not wholly for the balance sheets.

So, mostly, we seem unaware
Of what they're doing when they're there;
But quick enough, when they are not,
To pull them in to stop the rot.

The epitaph for such a plight
Is — 'rarely seen, till out of sight!'

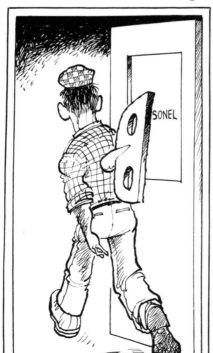

THE SALARY APPRAISERS

Salary Appraising
Is the art of crystal gazing,
Based on surreptitious viewing
Of what other firms are doing.

And with no one feeling able
To be bottom of the table,
They massage each other's notion
Of reciprocating motion;
So the magic wheels keep turning
For executival earning.

Thus we circulate the money
To the bees around the honey,
With diminishing gyrations
Into early liquidations!

THE HEALTH AND SAFETY MAN

Health and Safety men inspire
Images of Jeremiah,
With prophesies of doom and fire.

Classified among the spenders,
What they recommend engenders
Yawns on corporate agendas;

Until, that is, some new disasters
Energise their lords and masters
To action, when the time is past us!

The way to accident and sorrow
Is paved with 'bring it up — tomorrow!'

45

THE LADY EXECUTIVES

'There is — I hope I've made it clear —
No sex-discrimination here!
All our directors, if one checks,
Have mothers of the female sex,
Which should dispel what doubts persist
That we're in some way prejudiced!'

'Well, no! Not at the *senior* level!
We tried it once but — there's the devil! —
Between ourselves, these business ladies
Do ultimately want their babies!
So who are we, in such-like cases,
To keep them from their proper places?'

'Yes! *When* we get one on the Board,
Of course there's equal pay — Good Lord!'

THE SECRETARIES

If you ruffle up the feathers
Of the secretary-bird,
You may chill the office weather,
Though she seldom says a word;
But whatever is the matter
Will be signalled on the breeze,
By the angry pitter-patter
Of her fingers on the keys.

Which is why the word-processor
Is the bane of secretaries,
For not letting her express 'er
Irritation and her worries.

She's a special kind of logic, superseding your computer;
So don't wax too technologic, till you've checked that it
    will suit her!

THE RECEPTIONISTS

Up and down the hierarchy,
Heads of this-and-that exist,
But it's hogwash and mularkey
To the firm's receptionists!

When visitors creep through the door,
And take a hesitating pace,
It's not the Board they're looking for,
But 'welcome' on Reception's face.

So they're the ones who set the style
On which the whole damn show depends;
Not press-releases, but a smile
Which turns the strangers into friends.

A business, in the world's perception,
Is sitting there, behind Reception!

47

THE 'ASSISTANTS TO . . .'

The ones within the Corporate charts,
With whom we don't know what to do,
Or constitute unwanted parts,
We designate 'Assistants To . . .'

The more there are, the more we tele-
Graph the all-pervading view
That, by sitting next to Nellie,
Their real potential filters through.

What, in fact, the role infuses,
Other than the boss's tea,
Is 'Assistant To' confuses
Who's in charge, the boss or (s)he.

When corporate fleas catch smaller fleas,
It's Northcote Parkinson's disease!

THE OVERSEAS SUBSIDIARIES

Subsidiaries overseas
Do not comport themselves with ease,
Between the hosting-nation squeeze,
And owners shouting 'profits please'!

To make the profit's up for doubt,
But then there's how to get it out,
What with exchange-controls about
And sterling somewhat up the spout!

And management's a problem too,
For aspirants at G.H.Q.
Are not disposed to take the view
Careers are made in Timbuctoo!

Out here, we wonder what possessed us,
To join the overseas investors.

THE HOURLY PAID

The ones who make the wheels go round
In business, are not always found
At dizzy heights above the ground,
   Where all the power to vote is;
Their job's to work, without a fuss,
And adulate the likes of us
Up here, who never strike because
   No one else might notice!

It's all the Joans, and Berts, and Sids,
   Anonymously striving,
Who keep our status pyramids
   And hierarchies thriving;

And every Boardroom scotch-and-dry
Comes courtesy of lesser-fry!

The Stake Holders

THE SHAREHOLDERS

Bless us, Lord, and help us please
Our customers and employees;
But mostly, Father, heed our prayers
To please the Holders of our Shares!

Help our stock appease our friends'
Appetite for dividends;
And tempt them not to look afield
For some more scintillating yield!

Help the Institutions see
The promise of our equity;
And similarly well-dispose
The Pension Fund portfolios!

And silence AGM protesters,
Especially the small investors!

THE KEY ACCOUNTS

All customers are kings, they say,
But since Pareto rules O.K.,
The super-monarchy amounts,
In business, to the KEY ACCOUNTS!

For we know they know we know they
Know we know they'll get their way;
And they know we know they know why —
Since more of us supply than buy!

So, heads they win and tails we lose,
The KEY ACCOUNTS sit back and choose;
While we, and all our rivals, dice
With death to give the lowest price!

The only comfort for our curse
Is life without them's even worse!

51

THE BANKERS

'Go laughing to the bank' 's a phrase
We all enjoyed in former days;
But now is more or less bespoke
For bankers, as their private joke.

For though they'll charitably lend
Our Board a little more to spend,
It's mainly for the interest due
On what we owe to you-know-who.

The assets we perspired to own,
They have in hock against the loan;
Sure, should we succeed or crash,
They'll get the company or the cash.

Confucius say 'When bankrupt filing,
Only banker come up smiling!'

THE FEDERATION

While workers join the unions
To sanctify their stations,
Their bosses boast Masonic Clubs
Or favour Federations.

These friendly brotherhoods supply
A genteel kind of forum,
To guarantee competitors
Compete with due decorum.

For devotees of enterprise
Deplore unseemly schisms,
Like price disequilibrium
In market mechanisms.

So who — they ask in Federations —
Needs Anti-Trust or regulations?

TOMORROW — THE WORLD CORPORATION!

Tomorrow, and tomorrow, and tomorrow,
Creeps in this petty pace from day to day;
With profit less in evidence than sorrow,
As Business struts and frets along its way!

From yesterdays of primitive beginning,
On borrowed cash, and escalating loan;
With Everests of odds against him winning,
The business dreamer dreams his dreams alone!

Today, to ride the gales of liquidation,
And search for streams of sweetly flowing cash;
Become — who knows? — the Global Corporation,
With all the bankers' forecasts in the trash!

Transnational tomorrows, as it seems,
Were yesterday's least viable of dreams!

*The
Stake
Holders*

53

THE OVERSEAS AGENTS

For those untutored in the arts
Of business in some foreign parts,
A local Agent is the guy
To teach you what, and where, and why!

For agents' views of 'when in Rome'
May shock the auditors at home,
Who do not count the local gentry
As items in their double-entry.

Though they, like us, are men of honour,
Their business may depend upon a
Somewhat more elastic view
Of who slips what, and where, to who.

If their's is to import or die,
Then ours is not to reason why!

The Best of Boardroom Ballads

THE DECISION MAKERS

When we come to review
What the managers do
Which explains their superior rating,
We are told it is due,
And their salaries too,
To the size of decisions they're making.

And 'we won't' or 'we will's
A particular skill,
In the managers mainly residing,
Which the rest of the guys
In the management's eyes
Cannot match when it comes to deciding.

Which accounts for the flair,
And the infinite care,
The meticulous search for precision,
Which he daily deploys
In pursuit of the joys
Of the art of the business decision.

But the possible shock
Of his head on the block,
And a nasty response in The City,
May explain why he's prone
Not to go it alone
Till it's nicely diffused in Committee.

So some time may elapse
In the future, perhaps,
Till he rises above his defences;
And, unthreatened by blame,
Can quite openly claim
The applause for its best consequences.

And with so much at stake,
On decisions they make,
It has entered their innocent noddles,
To refer their distresses
To learned professors,
Computers and mystical models.

Now professors express
An intelligent guess
In the language of forecasting science;
And have found divinations,
Expressed as equations,
A hit with their gullible clients.

But decisions, my friend,
Are a means not an end
And it's 'how' more than 'what' that may matter
And the wise are, as ever,
More use than the clever —
Since there's more to decisions than data.

LADY ON THE BOARD

A Board Room is a kind of den
Wholly redolent of men,
Which women mainly get to see
When bringing in the lunch or tea;
But one or two, I would applaud,
Have brought a Lady on the Board,
Either out of great acumen
Or as their 'statutory woman'.

Either way, the eye detects
Unexpected side effects,
Which tend to make the Board Room rock
To massive metabolic shock,
And leave the gentlemen regretting
A problem of their own begetting.

For here the chauvinistic mind
Seems inescapably inclined
To place, in two main categories,
The ladies central to their worries;
Disparaging, behind their backs,
Their 'bomb-shell' or their 'battle-axe'.

The 'bomb-shell' image is a figure
Like Marylin Monroe's, but bigger —
Elegant, but only just,
Clothed about the thighs and bust;
Offering like Eliot's miss
Some promise of pneumatic bliss.

But contrary to male assumption
That pretty blondes have little gumption,
The modern version boasts degrees
Like MBAs and Ph.Ds,
And an intellect as real
As her physical appeal;

A combination which the men
Never hope to see again!

And, envy coupled with desire,
They watch the goddess rising higher
Until, with sunlight in her hair,
She occupies the Chairman's chair.

The 'battle-axe' implies a style
More dependent on her guile,
Since her feministic facets
Are seen as insubstantial assets.
Eschewing every pleasure known,
To which the weaker men are prone,
She maddeningly seems to know
Everyone's portfolio;
And, where information's power,
Accumulates it hour by hour,
Until, by process of attrition,
She decimates the opposition.

These ancient overtones of sex
Cannot prevent what happens next,
When every Boardroom stands ajar
To women as they really are —
Good and bad, like all the others
Of their gentlemanly brothers;
Revealing — and it really hurts —
The irrelevancy of their skirts!

THE BUSINESS CONSULTANT

Of all the businesses, by far,
Consultancy's the most bizarre!
For, to the penetrating eye,
There's no apparent reason why,
With no more assets than a pen,
This group of personable men
Can sell to clients more than twice
The same ridiculous advice;
Or find, in such a rich profusion,
Problems to fit their own solution!

The strategy that they pursue —
To give advice instead of do —
Keeps their fingers on the pulses
Without recourse to stomach ulcers;
And brings them monetary gain,
Without a modicum of pain.

The wretched object of their quest,
Reduced to cardiac arrest,
Is left alone to implement
The asinine report they've sent.
Meanwhile the analysts have gone
Back to client number one,
Who desperately needs their aid
To tidy up the mess they made.
And on and on — ad infinitum —
The masochistic clients invite 'em.
Until the Merciful Reliever
Invokes the Company Receiver.

No one really seems to know
The rate at which consultants grow;
By some amoeba-like division?
Or chemo-biologic fission?
They clone themselves without an end
Along their exponential trend.

The paradox is each adviser,
If he makes his client wiser,
Inadvertently destroys
The basis of his future joys.
So does anybody know
Where latter-day consultants go?

THE ADVERTISING AGENCY

Let us, if you'd be so kind,
Praise the triumph of the mind
Over more pedantic matter,
Which advertising Agents scatter
Around the edges of the green
Pastures of the Business Scene;
By which, as client fortunes roll,
Closer to the final hole,
They winkle, from the waiting hearses,
Ever mounting media purses,
For one more advertising burst,
Before the ashes are dispersed.

Words there are not good enough
To match the brilliance of the bluff;
Or adequately to explain
How businessmen of normal brain,
Enter Advertising Houses,
And leave without their shirts and trousers

The Agency Director who
Persistently performs the coup
Produces, for his rich commissions,
Unique Selling Propositions
Based, as decent Agents should,
On either Sex or Motherhood;
These are, to the Image Makers,
The Freudian Factors which will shake us,
From our apathetic tellies,
To buy some more to fill our bellies;
Or grab, to satiate our greed,
Still more junk we do not need.

Fresh in pinkish shirt and sneakers,
He bounds across the floor to tweak us;
While, busy at his heels, attends a
Retinue of unknown gender,
Heaped with story-boards and charts
And sundry other works of art.

JOUNCY JOHNSY,
JIMBLE, JANGLE,
AND JUNGLE
ADVERTISING INC

61

Soon the client's senses tingle
To the orchestrated jingle
Which, the test results declare,
Guarantees his market share;
And, by subliminal recourse,
To some Oedipean force,
Will open, through the hidden eye,
The full capacity to buy.
This time round he cannot fail
To finish with the Holy Grail;
Or see, although the budget's high,
His Sales performance hit the sky.

And on — through dinner at Le Beau;
Perhaps a little girlie show; —
Until our innocent of brain
Is popped discreetly on the train,
Not quite knowing, through the fun,
Who has lost and who has won!

The client's customers may be
A bit less gullible than he;
And more resistant to the guys
Who pulled the wool across his eyes.

IN CORPORE SANO . . .

The Body Corporate is prone
To some malfunctions of its own,
Too deep for therapy to foil;
And shuffles off this mortal coil,
Leaving the explanatory data
With the Company Liquidator,
And the shareholders in fear
Around the late-lamented's bier.

But, though post-mortems have their use,
There must be methods which conduce
Better to reveal propensities
To death in Corporate Entities;

And, better still, we need prognosis
Of arteriosclerosis,
And other prevalent diseases
Threatening financial seizures.

The more distinguished Company leeches
Start with anatomic features,
Placing, in exact location,
The organs of its operation.
The consequential chart, however,
Tends to beg the question whether
The brain and eyes, as often said.
Are really in the Corporate Head;
Or, by genetical distortion,
Somewhere in the lower portion.

This anatomic imprecision
Suggests the dangers of incision;
For a missed lymphatic cord
Might lobotomise the Board,
Or intended appendectomies
Produce Corporate vasectomies.
So, not-with-standing that it's rife,
Intervention with the knife
At the bottom, may not stop
Hallucinations at the top;
In spite of the seductive pleas
For amputation at the knees
As the favourite reliever
From the Company Receiver.

The Art of Corporate Prosthetics,
Without recourse to anaesthetics,
Bucks the metabolic issue —
The atrophy of Corporate tissue
Through wide-spread paralysis
By elephantiasis;
The most effective cure of all
May be to keep the Body small,
Starting with those wily foxes
— The Corporate Doctors.

THE BUYERS

Up, lads, up: 'tis late for Buying:
Empty pallets never thrive.
Inventories atrophying
Will not keep the firm alive.

Sales are up and stocks are tumbling;
Retail outlets press for more;
And the Works Director, grumbling,
Pounds upon the office door.

Wake: the vaulted warehouse slumbers,
Row on row of empty bays;
Lack of merchandise encumbers
What we need to pay our ways.

Up: the Company's depending,
And the whole production plan,
On the Buying Group's unending
Willingness to play the man.

Move: for Purchasing's a rover,
Must not leave them in the lurch;
Out, beyond the Cliffs of Dover,
Moves the never-ending search.

Up, lads: moping in your beer,
Contravene's the Buyer's creed;
China, Hongkong or Korea,
May supply the goods we need.

Duty calls in two directions;
Buy domestic where you can.
But your colleagues' disaffections,
May suggest a wider scan.

Prices keen and volume ample,
Access simple to the port,
Means that, subject to the sample,
Buyers to the world resort.

Wake: and multiply your contacts;
Probe the corners of the Earth.
And, with favourable contracts
Prove the value of your birth.

Wide the airborne army scatters;
Plastic food on plastic trays;
And, digestive tracts in tatters,
Telex through their flight delays.

Tentative negotiations,
Deep into the night they drag;
Hieroglyphics and quotations —
Till finally, it's in the bag!

See: the loaded trucks, returning,
Make the inventories leap.
Right, lads: now the wheels are turning,
There'll be time enough for sleep.

THE JAPANESE MENACE

From London to Bonn and Chicago,
In Zurich, Toronto and Nice;
Every island and archipelago
From Chile, to Holland and Greece;
Wherever Executive People
Slump wearily into their chairs
In the hope that the counting of sheep'll
Do something to lessen their cares;
Wherever the harrassed Director
Turns to sleep for relief when he can;
They awake to the frightening spectre —
Of Inscrutable Men from Japan.

Beleaguered in Basle and Benghazi,
The most robust of Corporate men,
Quake at the vast Kamikaze
Hordes of the murderous yen;
The ubiquitous bland Oriental,
No higher to most than their knee,
Turns giants of industry mental
To an unprecedented degree.
And the threat of the little invaders
Brings a strong, paradoxical urge
For yesterday's eager free-traders
To demand an embargo — or merge.

But it's not just the fact we're losing
The markets that's causing the fuss;
It's these damned funny methods they're using
Which they've clearly not borrowed from us!
Did you ever hear of employers
Giving life-time employment and such?
They're just doing these things to decoy us,
But the Board wouldn't care for it much!

So as for the dubious morals
Of having a National Plan,
With a MITI to sort out the quarrels —
Let's just muddle along as we can!

And a Japanese banker refuses
To behave as he should, we have heard,
By putting the money to uses
Our fellows regard as absurd.

In Bradford, Detroit and Lusaka
There are puzzled executives who
Pray that they'll learn in Osaka,
To do it the way that *we* do.

THE COMPUTER MEN

There was a time we just remember
When, January to December,
We would make, and pack and sell
And pay a dividend as well;
And most directors, good and bad,
Could multiply, subtract and add;
Or run their various Divisions
With time to take a few decisions.

But no one now would dare refute a
Message from his main computer,
Or embark on any caper
Without its thousand yards of paper!
The print-outs and the video-scan
Are quite enough for any man,
So no one really could expect us
To read the stuff *and* be directors.

The Monster answered us with queries,
Gestating through successive series,
And kept us busy days and nights
Like information phagocytes;
Until we thought we'd end the fuss
And make the damned thing work for us!
A process which, alas, consists
Of hiring Systems Analysts.

The Systems Analysts decreed
An urgent, over-riding need
For changing everything we'd got
To ease the information clot —
By relocating functions where
The King Computer would prefer;
Which made the hardware more contented,
But everybody else demented.

So now we have the finest data
Between the North Pole and Equator,
And the poorest market share
Discoverable anywhere!
Systems chiefs outnumber braves,
Crawling through the architraves,
With, to square the whole equation,
Vice-Presidents of Information!

We hoped that they might entertain
Our hyper-active Delphic Brain,
And might graciously afford us
Time for getting in the orders;
But now we're told the thing that's in is
Apples, micro-chips and minis.
No doubt soon we'll change to them —
Plus ça change, c'est plus la même!

CULT OF LEADERSHIP

Since first from earth's primeval slough
Societies emerged somehow
And, retrogressing now and then,
Produced the dominance of Men,
It has been commonly agreed
There must be people who can lead.

The prince, the father or the priest
Met some criteria, at least,
For making in the infant state
Their leadership legitimate,

Though often, too, the biggest stick
Determined who might make the pick.

And then to leadership's chagrin
Democracy came creeping in,
With radical ideas which said
The followers should choose instead;
Or, at least, should have a voice
To influence their masters' choice.

Except, that is, strange to relate,
Within the corporate estate,
Where leaders, we are told, instead
Leap fully-clothed from Zeus's head
Protected, unlike other things,
By some divine right of the kings.

Suggestions that the lesser fry
Have any right to choose defy
The consecrated rights of bosses,
Whether making gains or losses,
To answer only for their sin
To priests who put the money in.

And those who hew the wood and hump it
Are firmly told that they can lump it —
A system known to learned sages
To mark the neolithic ages,
But now unknown to observation
Outside the business corporation.

So leadership, as a result,
Is consecrated as a cult,
Endowed with charismatic powers
Light-years from the likes of ours;
Particularly useful while
The new machismo is in style.

So might it not be best to say
That leaders, too, have feet of clay,
And any claim to lead is hollow
Unless the troops consent to follow?
If not, I think the special pleaders
Should find another word than 'leaders'!

THE YOUNG EXECUTIVE

Since I was waist high to a flea,
Papa would take me on his knee
And, from time to time, decree
    The life that I should live;
I'd always thought I'd go to sea,
Or be a farmer such as he,
But he insisted that I be
    A Young Executive.

Acquaintance with my father's boot
Had taught reluctance to dispute
Suggestions he might contribute
    And so I acquiesced;
Requesting what might constitute
The Young Executive's pursuit,
And what it is they execute
    That had so much impressed.

Regretfully, Papa displayed
No detailed knowledge of the trade
Except that it was highly paid;
    And made the resolution
That I could also make the grade
And join the business-man brigade
If I sufficiently displayed
    Some gift for execution.

And so it was I came to buy
A natty suit and hat and tie
And felt that I was quite a guy
    When first I was recruited;
But now, at forty-five, I try
To understand precisely why
And what, before I come to die
    I've really executed.

If Fate would hand me back the dice,
Vouchsafing me to throw them twice,
I'd opt for something more precise.

I frequently have told her;
For I have come to realise
The Young Executive disguise
Insufficiently belies
   The fact of growing older.

But Old Executives, I've found,
Are rather thin upon the ground,
And why there are so few around
   Shakes my resolution;
For could it be that I am bound
To where a failed career is crowned
And ghostly Boardroom bugles sound —
   Last call for Execution?

THE MULTINATIONAL CORPORATION

When James D. Flaherty O'Rourke
Came from Dublin to New York,
And peddled round his hot potatas,
Few financial commentators
Forecast he was on the brink
Of World Wide Hot Potatas Inc.,
Founding his Global Enterprise
On Chirpy Chips and Handy Fries —
But such are the bizarre gestations
Of Multinational Corporations.

And having made the humble spud
Synonymous with motherhood,
And Chips With Everything the toast
Of every home from coast to coast,
He felt that he should not deny
The culture of the Handy Fry
To less sophisticated clients,
Untutored in potato science;
And ripe, on Wall Street's best assessment,
For World-Wide's overseas investment.

So soon the Hot Potata logo
Flew from Zanzibar to Togo,
With world-wide quality control
By satellite across the Pole;
Linking Chirpy Chip plantations
And process plants in fifty nations,
Including, after tense discussions,
A licence granted to the Russians.

The Tigris, Nile and Orinoco
Were switched from cotton, rice and cocoa
To propagation of the tuber,
As were tobacco farms in Cuba,
On the guaranteed assumption
Of escalating world consumption;
Till all the leading indicators
Were based on futures in potatoes,
With James the undisputed King
Of the carbo-hydrate Ring;
While OPEC in distress reviewed
The synthesis of starch from crude.

Wall Street analysts foretold
A flight from copper, zinc and gold,
And White House strategists demanded
Return to the Potato Standard.
Friedman joined the advocators
Of tight control of seed-potatoes;
And Downing Street was quick to see
Manipulation of P3
As the relevant equation
For final conquest of inflation.

But James was keen to leave decisions
On politics to politicians,
And moved with great reluctance to
Subvert a government or two;
Executives of Hot-Potatas,
Irrespective of their status
And the colour of their skins,
Daily disavow their sins,
Renewing oaths to Handy Fries,
To multinational enterprise,
And James O'Rourke's financial plan
For Global Brotherhood of Man.

THE SMALLER BUSINESSMAN

I am the Smaller Businessman,
In turnover, not stature;
The future now belongs to me,
Or so says Mrs Thatcher.
We are a million or so,
Awaiting our deployment,
And if we each take on a man,
We'll beat the unemployment.

I am the Smaller Businessman,
But wish that I were bigger;
I'm told that Small is Beautiful,

But Big is on the trigger.
And what between the interest
And loans for which I hanker,
I wish my dear old Mum and Dad
Had trained me for a banker.

I am the Smaller Businessman,
Getting somewhat smaller;
And after tax and V.A.T.
My creditors grow taller.
I've found some customers to buy
On terms including credit,
And so my income only grows
Pro rata to my debit.

I am the Smaller Businessman,
Not taking on much labour;
Unless you count the wife and kids,
And recently the neighbour.
I've found the almost perfect way
Of conquering inflation;
For, since I can't afford to pay
They do it for the nation.

I am the Smaller Businessman,
Thinking of expansion;
And it seems the only way
Is mortgaging the mansion.
So, with my new collateral,
I'll back my innovation;
But not get very far upon
A terraced by the station.

I am the Smaller Businessman,
Depleted but defiant;
I don't suppose I'll ever be
Conglomerate or giant.
But something makes me want to keep
My little business flying;
And if I never make the grade
It's not for lack of trying.

THE ENTREPRENEURS

The entrepreneur
Is increasingly rare,
But undoubtedly worthy of mention;
For the young of today
Understandably pray
For a regular job with a pension.

But a man with ideas
Now encounters a fierce
Irresistible pressure to scramble,
For a regular role
In some corporate hole
With a lesser temptation to gamble.

So the young and the bright
Who work on through the night
On the vision for which they may hanker,
Are unlikely to gain
Much reward for their pain
From the present day sort of a banker.

For the latter's inclined
To be more of a mind
To suspect innovations and think 'em
Less worthy to back
Than some dutiful hack
With a mortgage and regular income.

It's like slipping a disc
To be taking a risk,
If you don't care a jot or a tittle
For the maverick who,
With a favour or two,
Is a latter-day Ford or a Whittle.

And the money accrues
To the gentleman whose
Most consistent reaction is clear —
That an asset is such

As you count or you touch,
And you can't really touch an idea!

So the interest rate
Is enough to inflate
The rewards for the ones with the money;
And safely constrain
Any signs of a brain
With pretensions to dip in the honey.

But I don't have a doubt
That their talent will out,
Though the ludicrous system deters;
And I cannot conceive
That, in spite of it, we've
Heard the last of the entrepreneurs.

PUBLIC PRIVATEERS

It seems that virtue has, of late,
Not seven deadly sins but eight
To vanquish and eliminate
    To drink of heaven's nectar;
The most pernicious on the list,
Our leaders currently insist,
Is one the moralists have missed —
    The evil public sector!

But none, more wickedly than this,
Brings virtue to the great abyss,
Or poisons with its vampire kiss,
    Our economic vitals;
And prompts the righteous and the wise
To exorcise the evil eyes,
By sacred cries of 'privatise'
    To strengthen their requitals.

The new morality contains
Little to engage the brains,
But consistently sustains
    The ethic it's pursuing;
By which its druids blithely sell
The bits already doing well,
Which frees its acolytes to yell
    How bad the rest are doing.

Such fervent, self-fulfilling views —
Heads they win and tails we lose —
Are calculated to confuse
    The morally deficient;
Who, in their innocence, request
Why can't the public keep the best
And sell the market all the rest
    To make them more efficient?

But gods, the Delphic priesthood says,
Move always in mysterious ways,
And privatising that which pays
    Is in the holy verses;
While that which runneth at a loss
The Central Office omphalos
Decrees its devotees should toss
    To the public purses.

And so, to meet the Holy Writ,
We saw the branch on which we sit,
Or amputate the better bit
    With sacrificial axes;
Fulfilling, as the priest intones,
The message written in the stones —
That all the public ever owns
    Are burdens on the taxes!

THE HEAD HUNTERS

The man with foreign sounding name
Was on my line again today;
For quite a time it's been the same,
But how I wish he'd go away!

When first he called from Biarritz
I felt a trifle flattered;
And breakfast meetings at the Ritz
Made me feel I mattered.

But that was quite a while before
I gained my board promotion;
Yet still he tells me how much more
I'd earn across the ocean.

And judging by the dossier
Possessed by this recruiter,
I sometimes wonder if he may
Be hooked to our computer.

So on and on, with knowing winks
He dissertates about me,
And half-suggests my Chairman thinks
He'd do quite well without me.

And how he'd like to meet my wife
And, over dinner, urge her
To taste the oriental life;
And what if there's a merger?

I popped into the Chairman's suite
To exorcise my fears,
Before the fellow's indiscreet
Enquiries reached his ears.

And that has proved, without a doubt,
The proper thing to do,
For now I know the gad-about
Has lunched the Chairman too!

It seems our universal friend
Is quite a head-collector;
He's also sending round the bend
Our Managing Director!

So now I feel no need to hide,
Or feel at all affronted,
Recalling with a certain pride
The day my head was hunted.

At least I would if I were free
Of lingering suspicion
That our man of mystery,
May be the opposition.

My colleagues theorise he may —
This mutual friend at large —
Be KGB or CIA
Of business espionage.

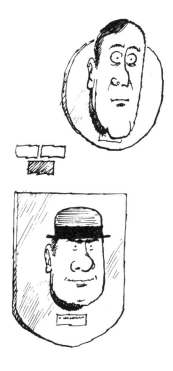

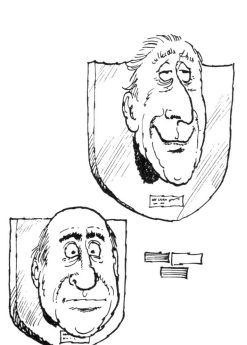

THE BANKERS

Oh to be in banking
Now that April's here!
And celebrate a spanking,
Profitable year!
Some prefer to hear a
Cuckoo on the wing,
But oh to be a Clearer
Now that it is Spring!

Better than the crocus
Peeping through the soil;
Richer than the hocus
Pocus with the oil;
Money is the medium
Surer than the rest,
For sweetening the tedium
With the interest!

Other men may hanker
For a bluer sky,
But oh to be a banker
Now the rates are high!
It's freezing, more's the pity,
The darling buds of May,
But down here in the City,
It's roses all the way!

Speak it not in Whitehall,
Tell it not in Gath,
Lest our little windfall
Cause Exchequer wrath!
Tell 'em it's for gearing,
A little more to lend
But mainly it's for cheering
Up the dividend!

Oh to be in lending,
Spreading joy around;
When every quid you're spending

Spawns another pound!
Loans are what we're here for,
Helping them invest,
Knowing they'll be back for more
To pay the interest!

Oh to be in Credit,
As the seasons turn,
With other people's debit,
Filling up the urn!
Never mind the weather,
Banking is the thing;
As long as we're together,
It's everlasting Spring!

THE DISTRIBUTORS

I pushed my trolley down the aisle,
Between the supermarket shelves,
And contemplated for a while
The eager shoppers help themselves —
As if in some hypnotic dream —
To frozen peas and clotted cream.

And, piling Pelion on Ossa,
Baskets bulging to the skies
With tangerines from Saragossa,
Deodorants and plastic pies,
They moved in ecstasy until
They reached the check-out and the bill.

Puzzled eyes, in consternation,
Watched the cash computers tick,
And struggled with the old equation
Of middle-man arithmetic —
How penny apples on the tree
Cost 30p. for you and me.

Observers of the business scene
Have clever answers to the riddle;
But to the customer they mean
The Law of the Extended Middle —
By which the price to them expands
The more the intervening hands.

The problem is they'd love to buy
The product free of all the padding —
The wrapping, brand-name and the guys
Who do the so-called value-adding;
And would so willingly dispense
With most of it to save the pence.

So maybe history was right
In placing at the very top
Of nations' economic blight
Their great obsession with the shop;
And, for every product sale,
An endless distribution tail.

So every item we produce
Sustains an office, shop or bank,
Squaring its hypotenuse
With costs and margins, rank on rank;
Turning my penny-worth of bacon
Into a pounds-worth of inflation.

But service-based economies,
The knowing and the wise insist,
Is where the richer future lies,
So maybe I should not resist;
I, too, will take the soft solution,
And keep my shares in distribution.

FRIENDS OF THE EARTH

We little thought that things would end
With OPEC seeming like a friend;
Or that we'd turn nostalgic eyes
To times when prices hit the skies,
And sing a eulogistic carol
For oil at forty bucks a barrel!

But then, at least, we stopped to think,
While teetering upon the brink,
That maybe there were ways to foil
The needless tyranny of oil;
And other methods worth the learning
To keep the wheels of commerce turning.

We even questioned was it worth
The raping of our Mother Earth
Or fighting never-ending duels
Like scavengers for fossil fuels,
And offering, in restitution,
A ravaged world and air-pollution.

And Nature seemed prepared to prise
The scales from our myopic eyes
And show what energies were there,
In wind and water, sea and air,
More rich, for those with eyes to see,
Than all the oils of Araby.

We thrilled to prospects of the union
Of man and nature in communion,
Harvesting the winds and tides
And energy the sun provides,
With some more promising equation
Between our needs and conservation.

While even those whose vision ends
With forecasts of their dividends,
Were galvanised by leaping prices
To seek alternative devices,

And place, upon a changing scene,
Their money where their mouths had been.

But economics, with their crazy
Politics of whoops-a-daisy,
Look as though they'll stand instead
Our expectations on their head;
And, with the price of oil declining,
Liquidate our silver-lining.

If energy renaissance needs
The impetus of others' greeds,
Let us, on our knees, implore
The privilege of paying more!
And may this masochistic pleasure
Teach us truly what to treasure!

UNIONISING THE MANAGERS

Should we, since the times are hard,
Get ourselves a union card?
And, with all our Boardroom brothers,
Organise like all the others?
Should we bite the corporate apple,
And pay our dues to join the Chapple,
Or seize our Battleship Potemkins
By courtesy of Brother Jenkins?

Should we managers unite
For the universal fight,
And cast aside our corporate chains,
We Bears-Of-Very-Little-Brains?
Rise, and learn the magic jargon
Of rule-book and collective-bargain?
Show the red in our corpuscles,
And flex our managerial muscles?

Emulate, without concessions,
Better organised professions,
By which the other social gentry
Practise their restricted entry?
Be like medicine or the law,
Who closed the shop and locked the door
And, basking in their sweet communion,
Told us not to join the union?

Should shareholders and workers seem
Much better placed to live their dream
Than managers who do not bother
To be the one thing or the other?
Why separate, but fail to be,
The devil *or* the deep-blue sea,
Playing our ineffectual fiddle
Like helpless piggies-in-the-middle?

Don't we owe it to the kids
To sublimate our hidden ids,
And lift the lid from our repression
About the prospects of depression?
Would it prejudice our morals
To collectivise our quarrels
And mutualise our apprehensions
About the safety of our pensions?

But would we ever heed the shout,
'Managers, directors — out!'
When there seem to be so many
Substitutes at two-a-penny?
Maybe we should keep our chairs
And hope for half-a-dozen shares,
Or some discretionary bonus
From our charitable owners!

CAREER CHOICE

Up at Cambridge, scraped a Two;
Stroked the boat and got my blue;
Wondered what on earth to do,
    With Greek and Latin verses;
Bummed about in Saragat,
Till father told me that was that,
I'd better be a diplomat
    And supplement the purses.

Sounded decent for a chap;
Commerce and related crap
Definitely off the map,
    According to the mater;
Pictured some idyllic scene,
Something out of Graham Greene,
In the service of the Queen,
    South of the Equator.

Met a fellow at the club,
Protegé of Pasha Glubb,
Mentioned Wadi-El-Khebub
    As a jolly station;
Phoned some Foreign Office guy;
Idiot suggested I
Had to be selected by
    Some examination.

Asked the johnny if he knew
Who-the-hell he's talking to;
Didn't know his Who-is-Who!
    Gave him quite a roasting!
Said he didn't care a damn,
For who's progeny I am;
Got to sit for some exam
    To get a foreign posting.

Finished up with little joy,
'Spite of being mummy's boy,
Disputing with the hoi polloi
    The diplomatic cloister;
Conceding to some tyke from Crewe
The posting out in Malibou,
And having Inland Revenue
    Suggested as my oyster!

Felt I'd had about enough!
Told the fellow where to stuff
All this bureaucratic guff
    For choosing whom they're needing;
Thought I'd pull a bit of rank,
Joined a City Merchant Bank,
Where they're more inclined to thank
    A chappie for his breeding!

THE UNDERSIDE OF ENTERPRISE

You know the game where eight or nine
People whisper down the line,
And 'reinforcements to advance'
Is 'twenty-four cents for the dance';
By the time the misbegotten
Message trickles to the bottom?
That's roughly how it grabs the guys
Underneath the enterprise.

And peering up the Tower of Babel,
From somewhere in the corporate navel,
Is apt to give the ones below
Communications vertigo;
As papers flutter down in legions
From pent-house to the nether regions
Producing, for the common herds,
A corporate flatulence of words.

And all this mangled up mularkey,
Cascading down the hierarchy,
Produces, quod est demonstrandum,
Asphyxia by memorandum;
Until what those on high intended
Is warped or otherwise distended,
With questions as to who's the wiser,
The doorman or the supervisor.

And as they multiply their sizes —
These Janus-headed enterprises —
And spawn division on division,
By dining on the opposition,
The aimless, disconnected sections,
Pursue their contrary directions,
Unable to resolve the riddle
Of what the head said to the middle.

So knowledge of the things that matter
Is roughly inverse to the data
Which shroud the monolithic giants,

Disguised as information science;
A state most frequently resulting
In fees for experts in consulting,
Grown fat upon the arcane arts
Of re-connecting corporate parts.

And as for the recurring myth
Of passing *up* the monolith
The views of these below the stairs
To those who breathe the upper-airs,
The evidence is in the scrawl
Of pained graffiti on the wall
Suggesting 'Antony was here!
Could anybody lend an ear?'

THE COMMUTERS

Except for those, of sombre mien,
Who ride the lonely limousine,
Or float to meetings, through the crowds,
On chauffeur-driven silver clouds,
Executive morale is seen
Most clearly on the eight-fifteen,
Where business-men, in diverse suiting,
Perform their ritual commuting.

For here it is the sales director
Rubs shoulders with the tax inspector,
And factory managers converse
With broker, City gent or nurse,
Across the usual divide
Which job and office may provide;
And free from the absurd inflatus
Derived from salary or status.

Across the carriages they toss
The things they never told the boss —
Not secrets of the way they're dealing,
But what it is they're really feeling;
What more pretentiously is meant
By gauging business sentiment,
By experts too refined to crawl
Like flies upon the carriage wall.

And yet, some sense and understanding
Of who's contracting or expanding;
And who are bears, and who is bullish
Or where the order-books are fullish;
Who's laying off and who's recruiting,
And which collapses they are mooting;
All this is traded, fast and free,
Across the plastic cups of tea.

And much is written in the faces
Of those who take more silent places,
And sit, between suburban stations,
Withdrawn from all the conversations;
Or, somewhat furtively and solemn,
Peruse the situations column,
And, animated now and then,
Make markers with a poignant pen.

The business microcosmic view,
Is in the buffet-car from Crewe,
Or riding the commuter line
From Maidenhead and up the Tyne;
And he who swaps the limousine,
In favour of the eight-fifteen,
May find some unexpected gain
Among the sages of the train.

THE POWER OF POSITIVE BLINKING

Since wishes, as the young are taught,
Are really fathers to the thought;
And thinking, for the businessman,
Is for avoiding when we can;
And since our board had had enough
Of all this corporate-planning stuff,
Finding that it didn't suit us —
All this messing with computers;
We all unanimously stated
Thinking to be over-rated!
Henceforth we would value higher
The use of corporate desire,
And decimate the competition
By force of positive volition!

Scarcely had we made a mention
Of our corporate intention,
And the news leaked out as well
Of our boardroom wishing-well,
Than press and television news
Pestered us for interviews;
And the brokers ran amock
Marking up the company stock.

Academic commentators
Rushed to validate the status
Of Management by Wish-Kinetics
As superseding cybernetics,
Locating the astounding credo
In the corporate libido;
And, in a rash of books, rehearsed
Which one of them had said it first.
While every business school was billing
Programmes in Collective Willing,
Claiming Shinto and Islamic
Sources for the Wish-Dynamic

Unions were quick to claim
Participation in the game,

Contented that the wages bill
Be settled by collective will;
And moved that plant negotiation
Be based on mass desideration.

And Government, whose every act is
Based on current business practice,
Lost but little time in hiring
The Head of Corporate Desiring,
From a well-known corporation,
To brief the Wish-Tank on inflation.

There is a move afoot, we hear,
To name us Business Of The Year.

INVISIBLE EARNINGS

No human heart, they say, can yearn
For what the eye does not discern;
Except, that is, down in the City,
Where the Invisibles Committee
Is stirred to hidden depths of yearning
By what we cannot see we're earning.

And floating, as their name befits,
Unseen, above our deficits,
They conjure from the upper air,
Just like the man who wasn't there,
Mysterious surpluses of trade
From products which were never made.

So, when the visibles are slipping,
Or sterling dangerously dipping
Into its periodic voids,
They calmly levitate from Lloyd's,
Or unseen royalties and fees,
The means to raise us from our knees.

Thus, month by month, they float the nation
By acts of prestidigitation,
Materialising from the skies,
Below the threshold of our eyes,
The cure for Treasury dejection
By extra-sensory perception.

I close my eyes to get a fleeting,
Dark illusion of them meeting
With vague, impressionistic spasms
Of men outside their ectoplasms —
A chairman, and his ghostly members
With poltergeistic non-agendas.

And, opaque as the general scene is,
They pull, like latter-day Houdinis,
Before our eyes see what they're at,
The earnings rabbit from the hat;
Then off! into the dark air gripping
Insurance premiums and shipping!

It seems the future of the nation
Is based on transubstantiation,
And economics of a kind
Where matter's subject to the mind;
The laws of metaphysics rule
In spite of what they teach at school!

They do say there be passing strange
Doings at the Stock Exchange,
Where, disembodied at the table,
They're non-corporeally able
To do extraordinary feats
With our invisible receipts!

ANNUAL GENERAL MEETING

The Chairman's great phlegmatic calm
Spreads its reassuring balm,
Like oil upon our troubled waters,
Throughout the corporate headquarters;
And soothes away our worried frowns,
Across the business ups and downs,
With words of fatherly good cheer,
For fifty-one weeks of the year.

But, sometime in the fifty-second,
On past experience, we've reckoned,
Even he will fall, instead,
Victim to some inner dread;
And brood upon the now impending
Prospect of the fiscal ending
And his ritualistic beating
At the Annual General Meeting.

With negligible dividends,
The annual event portends
A day of unremitting terror,
And pained acknowledgement of error;
When pension-funds and institutions
Exact their yearly retributions,
And vitriolic widows brandish
Their share-certificates in anguish.

While some, with well-rehearsed finesse,
And eyes upon the watching press,
Will make pejorative assessments
Of recent overseas investments;
Or use their half-a-dozen shares
To catch the Chairman unawares,
Enough to give the Board the vapours
When they read tomorrow's papers.

And how the shareholders will treasure
Their annual sadistic pleasure,
Or revel in this King of sports —
Delaying corporate reports —
Until, the final insult parried,
The annual report is carried!
And, off to gin and tonics boasting,
Oh, what a lovely chairman's roasting!

While he, poor soul, his torment ended,
Or for another year suspended,
A double-brandy on the shelf,
Is visibly his former self!
And offers, to relieve the tension,
In words I wouldn't care to mention,
A few, well-chosen apothegms
On shareholders and A.G.M.s.

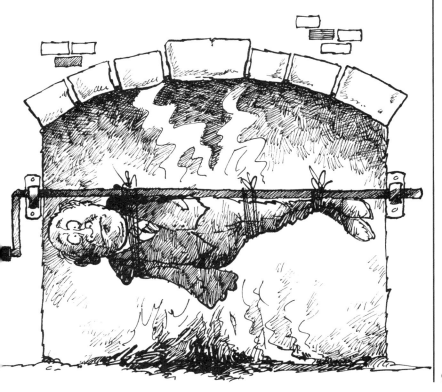

THE JOB DESCRIPTION

I trod, where fools alone may tread,
Who speak what's better left unsaid,
The day I asked the boss his view
On what I was supposed to do;
For, after two years in the task,
I thought it only right to ask,
In case I'd got it badly wrong
'Ad-hoc'ing as I went along.

He raised his desultory eyes
And made no effort to disguise
That, what had caused my sudden whim,
Had equally occurred to him;
And thus did we embark upon
Our classic corporate contretemps,
To separate the fact from fiction,
Bedevilling my job-description.

For first he asked me to construe
A list of things I really do;
While he — he promised — would prepare
A note of what he thought they were;
And, with the two, we'd take as well
The expert view from Personnel,
And thus eliminate the doubt
On what my job was all about.

But when the boss and I conflated
The tasks we'd separately stated,
The evidence became abundant
That one of us must be redundant;
For what I stated I was doing
He claimed himself to be pursuing,
While my role, on his definition,
Was way outside my recognition.

He called in Personnel to give
A somewhat more definitive
Reply, but they, by way of answer,

Produced some vague extravaganza,
Depicting, in a web of charts,
Descriptive and prescriptive parts
Of tasks, the boss and I agree,
Can't possibly refer to me.

So, hanging limply as I am,
In limbo on the diagram,
Suspended by a dotted line
From functions that I thought were mine,
I feel it's maybe for the best
I made my innocent request;
I hopefully await their view
On which job of the three to do!

ANYONE FOR TENNIS?

In the good old days we played,
Like decent chaps, the game of trade.
So, what the umpire said was that,
According to the rules of GATT,
Was taken, in the name of sport,
As ruling sanctions out of court;
And no ungentlemanly shout
Disputed when the ball was out.

But now, alas, the urge to win,
Has brought a breach of discipline;
With all the seeded players free
To desecrate the referee,
And go for game, and set, and match
By any rules their leaders hatch
Which give their overseas accounts
The better of the trading bounce.

For all the players it is vital
That no one else should win the title,
Though, what they can themselves produce,
May get them, at the best, to deuce;
So beggaring my neighbour's trade
Is how the winning lobs are made,
While players, point-by-point, dispute
Who brought the game to disrepute.

Americans, for whom it's sin
To play the game unless they win,
Are most inclined to hedge their bet
By doubling up the height of net;
This stops the European ball
From entering their court at all;
While Europe threatens to retire,
Or raise its own a sanction higher.

But both accuse the Eastern set
Of dirty play around the net,
And call the Japanese a menace
Unworthy of the game of tennis;
Or fight about the repercussions
Of playing doubles with the Russians,
In case the Eastern Bloc attack its
Service game with Western rackets.

The players, to a man, deplore
The ones who call the game a war;
Insisting it is only played,
Within the spirit of free trade,
By gentlemen who don't resort
To cheating in the name of sport;
It's simply not the game for fools
Who keep insisting on the rules!

DEMENTIA PRAECOX

Since fear is all we have to fear,
   As F.D.R. was prone to say,
I launched my corporate career
   By casting all my fears away;
Speak up, speak out! and, most essential,
Display your management potential!

So, in my best dynamic style,
   I shot my cuffs and banged the door;
And, with assured aggressive style,
   Walked tall across the boss's floor.
'Shut up, get out! I'm in a meeting!'
Was all he said by way of greeting.

I set a later time to meet,
    Perhaps a modicum deflated;
And practised yoga in retreat,
    To get my psyche re-instated.
Breathe in, breathe out! — and off once more,
Ambitious, through the boss's door!

'So, with respect Sir, I've concluded'
    (Was this my former, timid self?)
'Your whole damned strategy's deluded —
    I move you put it on the shelf!
You're in, you're out! Your profit's shrinking!
You need some new, dynamic thinking!'

The silence which ensued was total,
    Though the thunder in his eyes,
Through the threatening bi-focals,
    Left but little to surmise.
Then up! and out! — his voice pursuing,
With 'What the hell d'you think you're doing!'

So now I nurse my injured id,
    And feel a somewhat chastened fool,
Who tried to climb the pyramid
    My first day out of business school!
But work! and wait! — that's tough for me,
With 'A's in Corporate Strategy!

THE GHOST OF CHAIRMEN PAST

I loitered with a vacant smile
About the board-room gallery,
And contemplated for a while
Departed chairmen eyeing me —
A century of leaders, all
Impaled for ever on the wall.

Each beetled and majestic brow,
Sat brooding in its bed of oils,
And seemed anachronistic now
They'd shuffled off their mortal coils;
As if they'd nothing left to say
Of relevance to me today.

And mine, I knew, would be the face,
Within a year or two, no doubt,
To occupy the empty space,
When I no longer was about;
But could it really be that mine
Would be the last face in the line?

Whereat, to my eternal shame,
The founder, Thomas Binton, Bart.,
Leaned forward from his picture frame
And gave me quite a nasty start;
Suggesting if we sold to Carters
He'd have my rotten guts for garters!

And, animated up the room
The other faces, I re-call,
Attacked my prophesies of doom
With imprecations from the wall;
And then resumed their former places
Sedately in their normal spaces.

My board-room colleagues never did,
When next we all were congregated,
Know why we voted down the bid
I'd previously advocated;
But Thomas Binton, Bart., I think,
Gave me a reassuring wink.

And now I take my daily walk,
At lunch time, up the board-room floor,
And have a little private talk
With chairmen who have gone before;
I pray my own successor be
Insane enough to talk to me!

THE BUSINESS LITERATURE

They used to say, or so I've heard,
In the Beginning was the Word;
But since the television freed
Our species from the need to read,
The scriptures are assumed to mean —
In the Beginning was the Screen!
For books are strictly for the birds
Since images replaced the words.

Which makes it all the more surprising
That sales of business books are rising;
Though Whitman, Keats and Tolstoy burn,
Executive desire to learn
Has boosted by immense amounts,
On corporate expense accounts,
The means to mitigate distress
For owners of the printing press.

And half our literature consists
Of vast, interminable lists
On 'How To Ride the Product Cycle',
Or 'Severing The Umbilical —
What Every Corporate Doctor Knows',
In crude, impenetrable prose;
Till every office-suite is lined
With insights on the Corporate Mind.

Executives who find success
Are now obliged to go to press
With autobiographic ham
Or how I got to where I am;
While business-school professors stand,
Self-effacingly to hand,
To turn the home-spun exegeses,
Into an endless flow of theses.

Since what the commentators write is
Prone to polysyllabitis —
The virus known to me and you

As 'why one word when three will do?' —
The miles of paper, pulp and ink
Consumed on business double-think
Have brought the publishers reprieve
And riches they could not conceive!

This literature, it should be said,
Is rarely written to be read;
But adds distinction to the walls
Of corporate marmoreal halls,
Suggesting, by its acquisition,
A touch of business erudition.
So few are destined to discover
What nonsense lies behind the cover.

THE BUSINESSMAN'S DIARY

January: we explored,
At our meeting of the Board,
Why the year we'd just completed
Mustn't ever be repeated.

February: all agreed
Strategy is what we need,
To liquidate the Chairman's fear
On the current fiscal year.

March: unanimously moved
Action plan should be approved;
Especially in view of costs
Of three months we've already lost.

April: Finance Chief reviews
Prospects for our revenues;
Generally sad prognosis;
Sales Director under notice.

May: the Marketing Director
Senses he may now detect a
Movement in the market place,
If Production can keep pace.

June: the growth of finished stock
Suggests the forecast's all to cock.
Uproar as the meeting ended;
Half-year dividend suspended.

July: bank a little pressing;
Chairman ill and convalescing;
Plant on strike, but no one worries
Considering the inventories.

August: Marketing explain
New promotional campaign;
Quiet confidence prevails,
Possibly excluding Sales.

September: quarterly accounts
Suggest the wages cheque may bounce;
Chief Accountant wins reprieve —
Kept a little up his sleeve.

October: budget overspent;
Cut the price by ten per cent;
Advertising decimated;
Overheads re-allocated.

November: temporary pause;
Fire at main competitors.
Sales beyond all expectations,
Directors cancel resignations.

December: All the Board excited;
Rumours Chairman to be Knighted;
Letter to employees linking
Success with new strategic thinking.

BUSINESS MEMORANDA

When the Things from Outer-Spaces
Over-run the human races
And are sieving through the traces
Of the ruins which replace us;

Should they come across, at random,
Any business memorandum,
Do not fear! Nil desperandum!
They could never understand 'em.

For executival grammar
Would suggest a panorama
Where the writer tries to slam a
Piece of paper with a hammer!

Even Martians lack computers
So conceivably astute as
To decipher these polluters
Of our literary futures.

For the way the writer fidgets
With his syntax and his digits
Is enough to blow the widgets
Of the trans-galactic midgets.

Now their logical equation
Would assume that information
Is the prime preoccupation
Of this strange communication;

Whereas we who understand a
Businessman would never pander
To this vicious kind of slander
On his business memoranda.

THE CORPORATE MOTHER

Executives who meet together,
When the daily grind is through,
Rarely talk about the weather,
As other mortals seem to do;
Sex and business expectations
Dominate their conversations.

But, contrary to many critics,
This is not at all because
Businessmen feel aphroditic,
Wicked or promiscuous;
It's simply that their corporate lives
Reflect their mothers and their wives.

So, as with ancient navigators,
Dedicated to the sea,
Every artefact of status
In the corporate life's a 'she';
Hence comments such as 'down she goes!'
Describing Wall Street at the close.

So, that the dollar's feminine,
Or 'markets' are a female gender,
Is not indicative of sin,
But surrogates for something tender;
And 'matrix' structures are another
Subtle synonym for 'mother'.

American and European
Businessmen, albeit chaste,
Share a somewhat Oedipean,
Mother-oriented taste;
Their corporations, too, assume
Connotations of the womb.

For most executives of worth,
The deepest Freudian sensation
Is presence at a product's birth,
When all the traumas of gestation
Are sublimated in another
Offspring for the Corporate Mother.

DEATH BY MERGER

A corporate entity, which starts
As just an aggregate of parts,
Evolves in time, within its whole,
An idiosyncratic soul.

This personality defeats
Analysis by balance sheets,
The way your character eludes
The X-ray and the cathode tubes.

These tell us much about our health,
As balance sheets of corporate wealth;
But neither takes us very far
Towards clarifying what we *are*.

But what we *are*, on this strange earth,
Defines our value and our worth;
Not, for a man, his ears or throat,
Nor, for a company, its quote.

Yet analysts are prone to make
This odd but seminal mistake,
And think the rules of purchase hold
When companies are bought or sold.

But what the buying company gets,
So often, to its great regrets,
May be a useless bag of parts,
Like buying men without their hearts.

Financial analysts are, then,
The very worst of corporate men
To make so subtle a decision
As merger or as acquisition.

This may be why we see the trail
Of acquisitions, doomed to fail,
Abandoned to the Jack-the-Rippers
Of corporate life — the asset-strippers.

Above all, it's the people presence
Which permeates this corporate essence,
And catalyses, through the whole,
Its special chemistry and soul.

So synergies from mergers fail
Because the soul is not for sale;
Just as, when plants and factories close,
More dies than most of us suppose.

CORPORATE GAMES

The Chairman will, from time to time,
Most properly exhort us
To cast our beady eyes upon
Events across the waters;
So the focus for the moment,
And the flavour of the day,
Are the corporate dynamics
Of the great U.S. of A.

And what is it we mainly saw? —
A series of ferocious,
Supercalafragalistic-
Expealodocious,
Totally fantastic
And unprecedented surges
Of the most colossal, corporate
Conglomerated mergers!

So the Number One economy's
Most fascinating facets,
Were less about production
Than the swapping round of assets;
And everyone gyrated
To the predatory patterns
Of the bid and counter-bidding
Over cocktails and manhattans.

The bankers and the brokers
Were the beneficiaries

Of this burgeoning bonanza;
And the legal luminaries
Were the laughing legatees
Of all the endless litigation
Which titillates the palate
Of the hungry corporation.

So they, at least, seemed happy
With their dinosaur-like clients,
As they locked their horns together
In their battle of the giants.
But other people might prefer
Their corporations thinner,
And cheque-book competition's
Not the way to pick the winner!

Just one or two are asking
What became of Anti-Trust?
But, federally speaking,
No one seems too very fussed;
And we all are now adherents
Of the self-same orthodoxy,
So will, no doubt, contract their
Merger-mania by proxy.

THE EXECUTIVE COMMANDMENTS

There are three things
That executives do,
Which the boss tells me
I must now eschew;
I must not speak before I'm told
Or interrupt, or be too bold,
If I ain't gonna grieve
My boss no more!

So I went on a course,
Interpersonal skills,
For executives who

Have obtrusive wills;
I learned how never to aver
And how politely to demur,
So I ain't gonna grieve
My boss no more!

There's another thing,
That I should not say;
I should not presume,
To a rise in pay!
For if I raise too much commotion
I may jeopardise promotion,
And I will grieve
My boss some more!

There's a special thing
That I must beware;
I must never ask
How the Board got there!
I must not draw the wrong conclusions,
Make pejorative allusions,
Or I will grieve
My boss some more!

The important thing,
In the corporate race
'S not to self-destruct
But to self-efface;
And he who does not get frustrated
Will be highly compensated,
And he'll grieve
His boss no more!

There's a final thing,
In this crazy song,
I must not suggest
That the boss is wrong!
For when my boss is underground
I'll be the only boss around,
And you ain't gonna grieve
This boss no more!

EVERY DOG HAS HIS DAY

When things are tough, I while away
The traumas of the working day
Rehearsing what I'm going to say
   The day I take my pension;
And after forty years, or so,
I recommend my parting show,
For, brother, what a way to go
   And letting off the tension!

The scene: my main director stands,
My gold watch in his clammy hands,
And jowls like india-rubber bands,
   To give his valediction;
And, to applause, I say I think
It's nice to meet the Missing-Link
When not, for once, the worse for drink
   Displaying his affliction!

And then to everyone's delight
I ask the chairman, on his right,
To step outside the door and fight
   And get his due come-uppance;
Or would he rather I announce
His special numbered bank accounts
In Zurich where his cash amounts
   To somewhat more than tuppence.

And then by way of coup-de-grâce,
I empty on the silly ass
The contents of my brimming glass,
   To shouts of acclamation;
And casually tell the fools
There's going to be a change of rules,
I've won a fortune on the pools
   And bought the corporation.

But just as I'm about to call
The Board to meet and sack them all,
The voice next door begins to bawl
    That something needs revising;
A hundred times a day, it seems,
He interrupts me with his screams;
What good's a boss who spoils your dreams?
    So much for fantasising!

EDDIE 'BONZO' MORIARTY

Everybody, hale and hearty,
Crowded to the office party
Eddie 'Bonzo' Moriarty
    Threw to celebrate the three
Reasons for his feeling better,
Notably his morning letter
Saying he was going to get a
    Rise, and be the new V.P.

Sadly, the elated Eddie
Wasn't walking very steady
When the President was ready
    To confer the accolade;
Quite forgot the boss's chronic
Hatred, verging on demonic
Of liquids such as gin and tonic
    Stronger than a lemonade.

Unabashed, with joy unbounded,
Eddie tipsily propounded
How his new success was founded
    On the cult of scotch and gin;

Singing from diminuendo
To a staggering crescendo
Ballads with the innuendo
    That abstention was a sin.

And thus did Eddie's prospects slip
Forever twixt the cup and lip,
Where others, too, have made the trip
    Which beckons all and sundry;
For he who dares to tempt the fates,
Until secure behind the gates,
Should learn the latin saw which states —
    Sic transit gloria mundi!

TWENTY-ONE TODAY!

When I was one and twenty,
    And starting on my way;
And hopes were high, and plenty
    Of promise in the day;
The manager would tell us
    The future's with the young,
So come along, you fellers,
    And climb another rung!

To gain a reputation
    And mix it with the rest,
With prospects of a station
    Up there among the best;
Work was a beginning,
    Facing to the sun,
With everything for winning
    When I was twenty-one!

Now, my one lament is
   That things are not to be,
For current ones-and-twenties,
   The way they were for me;
I wonder how I'd face it,
   To sense I didn't matter,
And be a crude statistic
   In the unemployment data.

Better, on the whole, is
   To have known a job and lose it!
But a youngster on the dole is
   More than madness if we choose it!
And will we be the nation,
   When historians look back,
Who betrayed a generation
   To the dole queue and the sack?

Beggars can't be choosers
   Is the counsel of despair,
The philosophy of losers
   Too insensitive to care;
Time the young were getting
   Their places in the sun,
From those who are forgetting
   When they were twenty-one!

ORIENT EXPRESS

As producers of polythene plastic,
Our demand was a mite inelastic;
   For our business to miss
   The impending abyss,
Required something a little more drastic.

So we thought of a foreign adventure,
On the strength of our final debenture,
    To export expertise
    To the far Japanese
In a joint Euro-Nipponese venture.

Though their people were truly delightful,
Their devotion to duty was frightful;
    For the talks over-ran,
    In a room in Japan,
Two consecutive days and a nightful.

At the end of the talks we conceded,
They knew more about plastics than we did;
    So we flew back again
    With a bank full of yen,
In return for our plant which they needed.

And we now, every Tom, Dick and Harry,
Are a Japanese subsidiary;
    But it's clear that the plan
    We reversed in Japan,
Has prevented our mass hari-kari.

And we've found our new owners so far so
Polite, with their bows and their 'ah-so',
    With the singular quirk
    That they're gluttons for work
When required to reveal that they are so.

Yet it does seem a little ironic,
The employees we thought so moronic,
    Seem to think that the Japs
    Are just bloody fine chaps,
And the rate of production's a tonic.

And the sight of our board exercising,
Was beyond any human devising;
    But our spirits and verve
    Grow in line with the curve
Of our profits and revenues rising!

CHRISTMAS PARTY

Welcome to the Christmas jolly!
Came round fast again, by golly!
Even though it's plastic holly,
    Here's to yet another year!
    Come on in, you girls and fellas,
Hand around the panatellas,
Get the vino from the cellars,
    Take a glass or grab a beer.

Sorry that you missed your bonus,
Here's to all the City moaners!
Anyone prefer coronas?
    Fill 'em up and don't say when!
So, the situation's chronic,
All our customers moronic,
Pour yourself a gin and tonic,
    Consolidated floats again!

Cheer up, Charlie! Lord protect us!
Where's your faith in our directors?
Let's get out the new prospectus,
    Show a bit of business spunk!
Why not make that mausoleum
That you work in a museum!
Can't you close your eyes and see 'em
    Flocking in to see the junk?

Trust the brokers to ignore us!
Someone give us all a chorus,
Get old Parkinson to pour us
    All another glass of beer!
Everybody feeling better?
Told you we would never let a
Company Receiver get a
    Grip on all our Christmas cheer!

Right then! Lubricate your throttles,
Loosen up your epiglottals,
Lead us off with Ten Green Bottles,
    Never rains but what it pours,
Happy Christmas all you rowdies!
Down with pessimists and dowdies!
We could always call the Saudis!
    Here's to dear old Santa Claus!

More Verses
on the Office Wall

SMILING THROUGH

By temperament, the Businessman
Stays optimistic when he can,
And, in adversity, supposes
Everything will come up roses!

Wholly disinclined to whining,
Every cloud's his silver lining,
Even while — as may await us —
They're showing in the liquidators.

It matters not the bank has said it's
Cutting off his line of credits!
Guess who's factoring his debts
For one more fling to back his bets?

Always in tomorrow's mail
May come that one stupendous sale,
And chance to tell the bank — oh bliss! —
To stick what up which orifice!

Even as the business crashes,
He's rising, Phoenix from the ashes,
Confident, if none the wiser,
He'll sell the ash for fertilizer.

Before they've snipped the umbilical,
He's bouncing to the business cycle,
And, in his genes, already feeling
His destiny in wheeler-dealing.

For such a one, who in his sleep
Could sell the fleece back to the sheep,
There is no cure for this addiction
By bankruptcy or such affliction.

Life's a never-ending look
To find a deal and make a buck;
And when he's deepest in the ditch
He never doubts he'll make it rich!

So, up and off to seek the prize,
Our Valiant-For-Enterprise
Pursues commercial pastures new,
Incorrigibly smiling through!

OPPORTUNITY KNOCKS

Jimmy Johnson got the sack,
Flat redundant on his back;
Message straight from Downing Street;
Off your back and on your feet!

Made the unemployment crawl
Round the town. No work at all.
Department of Employment tyke
Says off your feet and on your bike!

Buys a bike and takes his chance;
Pedals like the Tour de France.
Swaps the blisters on his feet,
For blisters round about the seat.
Nothing! Home to change his socks.
Sees the Chancellor on the box.

Says he's all for market forces;
Off your bikes and on your horses!
Opportunities abundant,
Specially if you're redundant.

Jimmy rides, with blistered thighs,
Into private enterprise.
Tops his handshake with a loan,
Starts a business of his own.

Finds that enterprise consists
Of grocers and tobacconists,
Each with somewhat larger shares
Of creditors than customers.

Jimmy's cheque's about to bounce,
Hears the Minister announce,
Off your horse and use your hooter!
Get a personal computer!
Fill the form and get your grant,
Information's what you want!

Finds his faster flow of facts
Mainly V.A.T. and tax;
Main advantage, he admits,
Totting up his deficits.
Wonders if it's worth the pain,
Growing blisters on his brain!

Feller on the telly talking,
Says let your fingers do the walking!
Jimmy tells him, What the hell!
Blisters on my hands as well?
I've had 'em on my back, my feet,
My thighs, my head and round my seat,
My bike, my horse and micro-chips,
And now they want my finger-tips!
Must think we're all bloody fools!
I think I'll settle for the pools.

125

CHIPS WITH EVERYTHING

Why do they say the way to hell
Is paved with good intentions,
When every business person knows
It's paved with new inventions?

And three advances, out of four,
These gurus tell us matter,
Are less about producing more
Than processing the data!
So what we make, or what we sell,
And what the banker loans us,
We spend on keeping up with all
The information Joneses!

Now, first we mortgaged half the firm
To buy the big computer,
And stood the business on its head
To pacify and suit her;
But what with systems analysts,
And useless information,
The choice was kill the wretched thing
Or file for liquidation!

So then they said that 'big' was out;
The trendy thing that's in is
To do your own computer thing
With micro-chips and minis;
And status for executives
Is measured by the label
On the Sinclair in your pocket
Or the Apple on your table.

And still the data mountains grow,
Though now the system varies;
So why is it, the more we know,
The less our market share is?
It's garbage in and garbage out,
And VDUs compelling
More time to view instead of do
The managing and selling.

Now, just as we were feeling less
The antiquated novice,
They tell us what is à la mode's
The automated office!
And de rigueur, let no man dare
Before his priest-confessor,
To put about some secret doubt
About his word-processor.

So round the integrated circuits,
On the technoholic binge;
Micro-chips for tea and supper,
Chips with nearly everything.
Maybe we should *talk* a little,
Think, before the system flips;
Look, to try and find the people,
Drowning in the micro-chips.

'WHY CAN'T A WOMAN BE MORE LIKE A MAN?'

Funny thing! — that we are free
To think of 'manager' as 'he',
Even up against the stubborn
Fact that 'he' may be a woman!
Ipso facto, such a 'she' —
Pronouns being what they be —
Cannot, in the abstract sense,
Call one 'she' without offence!

In business, if we sign 'J.N.'
Presumption is, of course, we're *men*;
Conventions says it wouldn't do
For Jenny Noke to do it too!
And if it's 'they' — the thought conveyed is
Men, until we've proved we're ladies!

To compensate, by 'Ms' or 'Missus'
Risks chauvinistic prejudices;
While signing 'Janet Brown' too early,
Provokes, from some, 'presumptious girlie'!

It's thus that idiom contrives
A blight on women's business lives,
And subtle solace for such others,
As see them all as fallen mothers!

But language is, for all its flaws,
More like the symptom than the cause;
So 'womager' is not the answer,
Or similar extravaganza,
Such as some seek, to ease our worries,
By delving into dictionaries.

'Teacher' broke the sexist rule
Because we met them both at school;
And 'manager' will not evoke
An image, other than a bloke,
Until the chances are we'll meet
More women in our bosses' seat.
So, *opportunity*'s the thing,
And words just puppets on a string!

OH, WHAT A LOVELY WAR

I doodled on my memo-pad,
As is my kind of Freudian fad,
For coping with the over-heating
Which permeates our weekly meeting.

The dialogue was getting warm,
And running pretty true to form,
Undeviating from the text
Which guarantees what happens next.

We'd had the weekly testament
On how the budget's over-spent,
Along with our accountant's terse
Forecast of its getting worse.

Marketing had then propounded,
Its rhetoric of hope unbounded,
Tinged with but the single doubt —
That Sales must get their digits out.

Then, strictly to the text, it's Sales
Who next rehearse their weekly wails,
Depicting by a long tradition
Production as the opposition.

Sales then decently withdraw
To let Production have the floor,
Since, in the game of dog eats dog,
Each must have his monologue.

Production lays about it well
By castigating Personnel;
Who, by the rules, can then subscribe
Their lesson in the pointed jibe.

And when catharsis has resulted,
And all are suitably insulted,
With quarter neither asked nor given,
All is finally forgiven.

So each, with warm and friendly greeting,
Looks forward to our next week's meeting,
Eager to engage, once more
The inter-departmental war.

The doodles on my pad, I find,
Are drawn from my unconscious mind
And most resemble scenes that pass
For Alice Through the Looking Glass.

THE DIRTY HANDED TONS OF SOIL

Production men — it's mainly true —
Have lacked respect to which they're due;
As if to spend their time with spanners
Left slightly questionable manners,
Necessitating that they wear
A kind of cordon sanitaire —
Or so the attitude entails
Of some with cleaner finger-nails.

And further more, for what it's worth,
By very nature of his birth,
An engineer was thought to be
From social classes two or three,
So not, like some among his peers,
At Eton in his former years;
Hence lacking in the social graces
Required for elevated places.

Too long, we chose to favour trade
To what is actually made;
As if to handle a machine
Were, in some curious way, obscene;
While finance, stocks and shares, or shipping
Were oh! so marvellously ripping!

Though now we hear our daily sermons
To emulate the Japs and Germans,
They both quite palpably pursue
The totally opposing view.
We talk technology with feeling,
But status goes with wheeler-dealing.

PASSION IN THE CITY

Down in the City something's stirring,
Most unlikely partners pairing,
Jobbers, brokers, bankers sharing
    In the rapture of romance;
Clearers, merchants and insurers
Raise their passionate bravuras,
While the Stock Exchange procurers
    Lead the orgiastic dance.

Institutions, hell for leather,
Leaping into bed together,
Post the banns and tie the tether,
    Bigamy no bar to sex;
City men in stripey trousers
Hang around the Discount Houses,
Propositioning for spouses,
    Brandishing their furtive cheques.

Lambs are lying down with lions,
Propagating monstrous scions,
Cartelised by mis-alliance,
    While the City Watch-Dog beams;
Now's the merry month for mating,
Season of de-regulating,
Bids and mergers consummating
    Fantasies beyond their dreams.

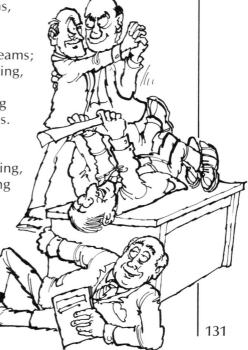

In among the heavy breathing,
Frenzied foreign limbs are heaving,
Adding to the shapeless, seething
    Paroxysm of their greed;
Lovely orgy! Such a pity!
In their fun they raped the City,
Carved her into not-a-pretty
    Parody of what we need!

131

THE UNMENTIONABLE PENSION

The interview, by which to get
A first appointment, is beset
With complex rules of etiquette
Which aspirants should not forget

Avoid, for instance, any mention,
Whatever be your apprehension,
About the details of the *pension* —
This might create an air of tension.

There's nothing like the pension point
For putting noses out of joint
With those whom companies anoint
With power to choose and to appoint.

For, if you're made of proper stuff,
It should be patently enough
To risk the smoother with the rough,
Without such after-sixty guff!

Ambition and commitment call
For showing no concern at all
For what would happen if you fall,
Or who would keep the wherewithal!

Such attitudes and questions give
Some altogether negative
Suggestions that the way you live
May not be quite executive.

Indicate you're quite unfussed
At what would happen, if it must,
Should the company go bust;
To think of it's a breach of trust.

Remember, too, such questions phrase,
In sensitive and painful ways,
What, to his cost, in former days,
Your interviewer failed to raise.

THE BUSINESS OF BUSINESS AWARDS

Pro Bono Publico, they say,
Distinguished folk receive their K;
The literati strain their eyes,
Unsleeping for the Nobel Prize;
And actors sublimate their inner-
Angst to be an Oscar winner.

Maidens manifest their vitals,
Manic for their Miss World titles;
Athletes weep without decorum
When voted Victores Ludorum;
And politicians change their dates
For Honorary Doctorates.

The question is — what equal prize
Gets Business temperatures to rise,
With boss to door-man pumping in
Emotional adrenalin?
Some great collective 'We're the Best!'
That gets us puffing out the chest?

OK, we've got the Queen's Awards,
And chairmen kneeling under swords;
We've Business Persons of the Year —
All worthy of a decent cheer.
But what we need's some great big thumping
Call, to get the whole firm jumping!

MID-CAREER CRISIS

Since tottering from mother's knee,
It's been the business life for me;
I made the board at forty-three,
And thrive, executivally!

So why am I a schizophrene
Whose alter ego's not so keen,
And dreams of other pastures green,
Out there, beyond the business scene?

Are other businessmen without
Seditious thoughts of dropping out,
And raising chickens in devout
Silence in some far redoubt?

Is it best that one ignores
These fantasies of further shores,
And diagnoses as the cause
Executival menopause?

Or is it time to cut the tension,
Damn the status and the pension
Paralysing my intention —
And leap into some new dimension?

THE CHINA SYNDROME

Business leaders in the West,
Occasionally find it best
To keep their cards close to their chests,
To guard their future interests.

And so their formal statements throw
Less light on how they plan to grow,
Than what their travel agents know
From where they've been or plan to go.

When chief executives migrate,
Their destinations designate,
More surely than the hand of fate,
The markets they anticipate.

Right now, on Jumbo-jet and liner,
They're cramming every bar and diner,
From London, Bonn and Carolina,
On the pilgrimage to China.

The presidents are dropping in,
Like plagues of locusts on Pekin,
And toasting, with embarrassed grin,
Their hosts in Pidgin Mandarin.

Directors, who can scarce recall
Occasions when they walked at all,
Are on the mandatory crawl,
Up and down the China wall.

Blistered feet are but the price,
Like using chopsticks with their rice,
To melt the oriental ice
And guarantee the gains suffice.

Where Marco Polo first began as
Advocate of Western manners,
They're off to wave their business banners,
Egged on by their corporate planners.

It's not so long ago they ran
Like leaping lemmings to Japan;
And, just before, the caravan
Was mainly moving round Iran.

This time, let's hope they've got it right,
With decent dividends in sight . . .
Meanwhile, where chairmen choose to fly,
May tell us more than meets the eye.

CREATIVE ACCOUNTING

When I was wet behind the ears,
And innocent, in former years;
Not really knowing — would you credit? —
My trial balance from my debit;
I held the simple-minded view
That one and one were always two,
And what was basic to accounting
Was truth, and aptitude for counting.

But nothing, I now know, encumbers
The poor accountant more than numbers,
Since sentiment among some clients
Made budgets more an art than science;
Or what they call, with losses mounting,
'Creative' methods of accounting,
Which means, in euphemistic diction,
Accounts with elements of fiction.

Now, having studied my pursuit
In classes at the Institute,
I've never coveted, for sure,
The Nobel Prize for Literature;
And too much 'creativity'
Is not at all the scene for me!
I'll stick to my old-fashioned talents
For balances that truly balance!

THE NON-EXECUTIVES

Among the business oddities
　　With which we learn to live,
Is the notion of directors
　　Who are 'non-executive';
For in ordinary language,
　　It's a curious pursuit,
If we execute a function
　　Which we then non-execute.

Which is why the more enquiring
　　Have been anxious for a clue
As to what our non-executive
　　Directors really do;
While the idle look with envy
　　At the prospects of a thriving
Opportunity for earnings
　　By more non-executiving

There are two kinds of incumbent;
　　First the one whose sole intent,
Is to ease the bank's neurosis
　　On the way their money's spent;
And compliant with the Chairman's
　　Hesitation to be cluttered
With a bounder who may bite the hand
　　By which his bread is buttered.

But the second is a treasure,
　　Who regards his odd position
As expressly calculated
　　To bring wider breadth of vision;
They're a rare, protected species,
　　Non-executives who dare,
Tell their patrons, if they need it,
　　When to go to *you-know-where!*

WALL STREET BUBBLE

When Wall Street bears repair to bed
And wake up rampant bulls instead,
We know, though lesser men may cringe,
The stock exchange is on the binge!

And wide the happy breed of brokers,
Nature's quintessential jokers,
Sees some vision which transcends
The rest of homo sapiens.

Sentiment is what occasions
Stock exchange hallucinations
Adding dollars to the stocks
Of corporations on the rocks.

And oh! what economic japes
For punters on the ticker tapes,
To have their periodic caper
On markets only made of paper!

If only all the human race
Inhabited this magic place,
Where productivity and work's
Simply for the social jerks!

Apparently it little matters
That half the trading world's in tatters;
It's what the Wall Street gurus feel
Which turns the economic wheel.

Where stocks are traded in New York
Recovery consists of talk,
And life is seen in parallax,
Unencumbered by the facts.

The future we were keen to find
Lay dormant in some broker's mind,
Until he ordered us to 'buy'
And sent the market through the sky.

But champagne and the broker's laughter
Means aching heads the morning after;
And Wall Street with a pounding head
Is prone to change to 'sell' instead.

Why can't we all enjoy their trips?
Let's pay the unemployed in chips!
Then everyone can join the beano
On the stock exchange casino!

MANAGERIAL ACTION MAN

For managers of Bloopers Inc.
It's out of bounds to sit and think;
Thinkers are a load of trouble.
Make us all uncomfortable!

What we want are men of *action*,
Free from cerebral distraction!
Always running, never walking,
Guys who never tire of talking!
Communication's how you win it,
About a thousand words a minute!

Just sitting back to think and plan —
That's not for Bloopers Action Man;
All silent introspection's sin!

'Who let those liquidators in?'

ANCIENT AND MODERN

Poets, in the great tradition,
Had strange, apocalyptic vision,
By which they frequently foretold
Our futures, from their times of old.

The comic Aristophanes
Undoubtedly was one of these,
And though two thousands years away,
Uncannily describes today.

We still intone the same old words
He showed were nonsense in the 'Birds';
And in the 'Peace' the views he fleeces
Survive in Whitehall press releases.

But Businessmen should savour too
The benefits of déjà-vu,
Since Aristophanes provides
A feast of modern corporate guides.

He warns the board about fixation
On management by litigation,
Since they, like us, had made the court
A place of favourite resort.

He castigated Athens' ruin
By 'legal fees and counter-suin' '
And asked for better growth than more
Receiverships and Schools of Law.

And what about the poor producers,
When 'services' and 'trade' seduce us?
We can't all live, for goodness sakes,
Distributing what no one makes.

I strongly recommend a diet
Of 'Frogs' or 'Birds' when things are quiet,
If only to confirm the law
That life has been this way before.

THE CROSS-CULTURE KICK

I joined the business in the days
When people went their different ways;
And no one cared a damn for quirky
Folk outside of Albuquerque.
They were they, and we were we,
The way it was supposed to be!

But then we grew, to our surprise,
Into a global enterprise;
Discovering that Greece and Turkey
Have cultures unlike Albuquerque;
And buyers out in Bangalore
Think steaks are not what cows are for!

So now we've learned that he who goes
To rub a nose with eskimos;
Or cares to raise in Tonga-Linga
What locals think the proper finger;
Acquires, not only, in the end
The bigger corporate dividend,
But something rich we never knew —
These foreigners are *people*, too!

CREATIVE SHOOT-OUT

'Shoot-Out in Manhattan's not
Some macho-movie you forgot;
It's New York's picturesque description
Of Advertising's new addiction.

The battle for the big accounts,
Worth uncomputable amounts,
Is settled by a logic we
Might question in the chimpanzee.

The agents — often six or seven —
With names like Bumbleblatz and Bevan,
Rush forward at the client's inviting,
To touch their pens, and come out fighting.

Then each, with hopes beyond its dreams,
Assembles its creative teams,
Straining to outdo the rest,
At proving Blooper's Soap Is Best.

At last the client calls the hour
And — each from his secluded bower —
The ad-men come, with blazing scripts,
Shooting wildly from the hips.

Seven came, consumed with lust,
Six have bitten on the dust;
But one proved worthy of the quest,
To get to prove that Blooper's Best.

Thus do advertising clients
Scale the pinnacles of science,
And satisfy the doubts of any
Who thought they merely tossed a penny.

THE VISIONARIES

The businessman, it sometimes seems,
Is not supposed to have his dreams;
The bottom line, the profit plan,
Delineate his moral span.

The businessman with breadth and vision,
Is viewed like those who preach religion;
Be pragmatic! Live today!
Is more the Kosher business way.

Yet I have met, as may be you,
The businessman of broader view;
Who thinks there's something he's about,
That puts the narrow view in doubt.

To take decisions, hold the key
To other people's destiny,
Implies a contract more profound
Than ordering another round.

Now you prosper, now you don't
Is not the right of those who won't
See that what they choose depends
On more than year-end dividends.

Give me men about me who,
Aren't afraid to join the few
Who choose to take the other view,
That business needs its vision, too!

The profit and the bottom-line
Are not, to such a man, divine;
But just the elemental need
From which some mission can proceed.

Returns on assets, he'd contend,
Are just the means and not the end;
The bricks, the shovel or cement,
But not the finished monument.

And what the monument becomes,
A palace, or the worst of slums,
Is ultimately fashioned by
Some vision in the builder's eye.

And so it is that some explore
The question — what is business for?
There are a few who do not seem
Afraid of vision, or to dream!

TRANSATLANTIC QUADRILLE

Will you, won't you? Will you, won't you?
  Help the western world a bit?
Just a little White House something
  To reduce your deficit?
Presidential orthodoxy
Propagates the dreaded poxy;
Economic death by proxy
  Seems to be the size of it?

Can you, can't you? Can you, can't you?
  Get the base rate down a mite?
Get the Treasury together
  With the Fed and stop the fight?
When the mighty U.S. sneezes,
Everybody gets diseases,
Threatening financial seizures
  And the economic blight.

Can we, can't we? Can we, can't we?
  As your partners, ask you why
The dollar's like the lark ascending
  Higher than it needs to fly?
Shouldn't we be asking whether,
If we got our acts together,
We'd enjoy the better weather
  Someone forecast at Versailles?

Will we, won't we? Will we, won't we?
  Disengage each others throats,
When common suicide by drowning's
  What the present path connotes?
We and you will be connivers,
In a wreck without survivors,
If our disageements drive us
  Up the creek without the boats.

THE EXECUTIVE WIVES

Though executive wives live exemplary lives
　　In unstinting support of their spouses,
It's the frequent, sporadic outbursts of nomadic
　　Behaviour where most of her grouse is.

When she's settled for Rye, and the W.I.,
　　And the kids settled down to their topics,
One can only suppose that it gets up her nose,
　　To be yanked off again to the tropics,

But she'll go like a sport to some filthy old port
　　At the ultimate ends of the ocean,
And swallow her dread of the bugs in the bed
　　That attach to her hubby's promotion.

So executives' wives are their richest resources —
Except for the ones who prefer their divorces.

MORE EQUAL THAN OTHERS?

For half a century, at least
The business tide flowed West to East,
And business schools and commentators
Took their future indicators
From what was happening today,
    Somewhere in the U.S.A.

But recently, as it would seem,
Americans misplaced their dream;
And, for the painful time it takes,
Before the sleeping giant wakes,
Their more perceptive people preach
    The need to learn as well as teach.

And so, beyond their loud brigades,
Who advocate the barricades,
Or beat the isolation drum,
The signs of better days to come
Are in a new, more open view
    Of what we others did, and do.

So, for the rest of us, we must
Respond more freely to this trust,
And show them what we really are —
Not poor reflections from afar
Content to emulate their ways
    Through mid-Atlantic MBAs.

The time is ripe to clear the fog,
Through some, more equal, dialogue
Where they, like us, require the best
Of West to East and East to West;
And neither seeks to be another
    Craven image of the other.

The point is in the difference,
Which those who sensitively sense
The future promise from the past,
Feel blowing in the wind at last,
The U.S. message that it carries
    Is first — but primus inter pares!

THE MEDIUM IS THE MESSAGE

The more the media expand
The less we seem to understand;
The more the information flow,
    The less we really seem to know;
The more the messages we send,
The less we seem to comprehend;
Communication rules, OK?
    Although there's nothing much to say.

The future's Channel Four and cable,
Computers on the kitchen table,
With instant data through the night
    By video and satellite;
Let your fingers do the walking,
For who needs dialogue and talking?
Telstars in the bedroom presage
    The age when media *are* the message.

With instant data on the wall,
Who needs the power of speech at all?
And touch to activate retrieval
    Makes words unnecessary evil.
At last our progeny are freed
From any need to write or read,
Delivered from the old, absurd
    Tyranny of book and word.

Nor will there be much future cause
For venturing beyond the doors,
When Mum can get the beef and mutton,
    By simply reaching for the button;
When Dad can stay at home and sell,
By Satellite and Intertel;
And even Johnny's need to know
    Is programmed on the video.

The more the messages we're screening,
The more the message lacks a meaning;
The more the plethora of data,
    The less the meaning seems to matter.
Maybe — if we could bequeath a
Few less pictures on the ether —
Future ages might regain
Some space to exercise the brain.

LET THEM EAT CHIPS

Taking horses to the water
    Gives no guarantee they'll drink;
Equine modes of misbehaviour
    May be wiser than we think.
Take the white hot revolutions
    Humans seem to hanker for;
'Chips with everything', for instance,
    Just to change the metaphor.
Micro-chips were what the future
    Most of all depended on;
Unimagined dawns were breaking
    In the Vales of Silicon.
Every future was a function
    Of the messages we cram,
As with saints upon a needle,
    On to each successive RAM!
Chew the chips, spew out the people,
    That's the economic law,
Feed 'em integrated circuits,
    Stop 'em asking what it's *for!*
All aboard the next invention!
    Mount the magic kangaroo!
One more mighty leap for science
    Up the unemployment queue!
Even at the fount of knowledge,
    Wise men have been known to pause,
Breathalyse their technoholics,
    Till they emulate the horse.

NEW FASHIONS IN MANAGEMENT

Businesses, it seems to me,
Defy most scientific laws,
Including that of Gravity;
But Newton got it wrong because
He lamentably failed to see,
With apples falling round his crown,
That products of the *Corporate Tree*,
Fall mainly up and rarely down!

By processes which never stop,
Inexorable as the waves,
It pushes people towards the top
Till chiefs out-multiply the braves.
And this unprecedented fructure,
Special to the business sectors,
Produced the *Horizontal Structure*,
Where even tea-boys are Directors!

The time then quickly comes, of course,
In line with hierarchic sense,
To barricade the Boardroom doors
And thin them out, without offence.
For which the current favoured wheeze,
To supplement 'Assistant To . . .'
Are structures known as *Matrices*
Obscuring who reports to who.

The *Matrix* is a means whereby,
The status-seekers field of sight,
Instead of focussed up on high,
Is channelled more to left and right.
And current thinking, I've observed,
Is jobs, however trivial,
So long as *status* is preserved,
Seem more or less convivial.

There are, then, numerous correctives —
Product Centres, Project Teams,
Humble's Management Objectives —
To neutralise ambitious dreams;
The remedies, in great profusion,
Thick upon the ground as flies,
Indicate the same conclusion —
When in doubt, re-organise!

The opportunities are full,
Most behaviourists agree,
To counteract the massive pull
Up the Corporation tree.
But all this putting out of shoots,
Around the middle and the top,
Makes me wonder if the roots
Are strong enough to feed the crop.

EYE OF THE BEHOLDER

In the Country of the Blind
They say the One Eyed-Man is King;
But we, for leaders, much prefer
The few who cannot see a thing!

Or, possibly, they've second sight,
Beyond our normal seeing eyes,
Which makes the winter we perceive,
Eternal summer in their skies.

Only to their inner priesthood
Are such revelations due;
Not the uninitiated
In the unemployment queue.

Some may talk of liquidations,
Enterprises in their throes,
But these are wicked deviations
From official Vie en Rose.

What's the story mother told me?
Would that I were one of those
With the vision to behold the
Holy Emperor's New Clothes!

Lamentably more perceptive
Views on this phenomenon,
Would suggest our dear, elective
Highnesses have nothing on.

THE HOUSE THAT JACK BUILT

More
Verses
on the
Office
Wall

Where are the hands that made the wheel
That turned the lathe and shaped the steel,
And helped a thriving nation feel
   Proud of the house that Jack built?

Where are the brains that led the West,
Industrialised before the rest,
And made us feel that Britain's best,
   Because of the house that Jack built?

Where are the girls and where the boys,
With buoyant step and eager poise,
The promise of our future joys,
   Here in the house that Jack built?

Where are the hearts that used to care
For sick, or old, or in despair,
And say there's room for you in there,
   Safe in the house that Jack built?

Where are the arms that fished the sea,
That built the ships and kept us free,
And made the future seem to be
   There in the house that Jack built?

Where are the minds that could contrive
The spinning-wheel, the jet, the drive
That made it good to be alive,
   And live in the house that Jack built?

Here are the arms, the minds, the hearts,
The kids, the hands, the brains, the parts,
The skills, the hopes, the needs, the arts,
   Still in the house that Jack built!

Where are the wise, the leaders who
Will call for what they crave to do,
To build the house and build it true,
   Just as the other Jack built?

155

EXECUTIVE STRESS

I observe, in the press,
　　Embarras de richesse
Of ideas for relief
　　Of executive stress.
And, with each diagnosis,
　　Some further prognosis,
On optimum means
　　Of a metamorphosis.

Some believe in mens sana
　　In corpore sano,
And the marathon jog
　　By the Thames or the Arno;
Till the rampant corpuscle,
　　And ache in the muscle,
Put paid to the pains
　　Of executive hustle.

While others, I find,
   Are more strongly inclined,
To some Freudian view
   That it's all in the mind;
And executive gloom
   Can be traced to the Womb,
Or the Ego and Id,
   As they elbow for room.

But until we exhume a
   True cure for the tumour,
I recommend massive
   Injections of humour;
The kind we can give —
   Laughing not at, but with —
As the most therapeutic
   Incentive to live.

When a smile meets a trauma,
   It's mainly the former
Which tends to prevail
   Where the atmosphere's warmer.

THE AGES OF MAN

To Shakespeare, in the eyes of heaven,
The Ages of a Man are seven;
But businessmen, it's clear to me,
Are limited, at best, to three.

What Chairman you have known, in truth,
Went 'mewling, puking' in his youth?
Did Arnold Weinstock ever trail
To school 'unwilling like a snail'?
What member of the C.B.I.
Wrote sonnets to his mistress' eye?
Or banker, as suggests the Bard,
Was ever 'bearded like the pard?'

No! Businessmen, we may deduce,
Leap pin-striped from the head of Zeus,
Straight into the business cycle
Directly from the umbilical!
Without the time, where time's the essence,
For infancy or adolescence,
Or other stages of gestation
So low on capital formation.
For them, the life the gods decree,
Divides, like Caesar's Gaul, in three!

The first's the Henry Ford fixation,
Technology and innovation;
In which our hero dreams that he
Will make it with his Model-T,
And leap from garden shed to mansion
By multinational expansion,
With customers and City cheering
His global feats of engineering.

The Second comes when he perceives
That he who manufactures, grieves;
And fixed investments are for fools
Obsessed with factories and tools;
Who, blind to bankruptcy's seduction,
Erode their assets in production.
No! They who clearly have it made,
Are they who do not make, but trade;
And fortune, free of retribution,
Means services and distribution.

The Third — and transcendental — phase
Reveals what business really pays;
The bears that mainly find the honey
Are not in goods, or trade, but money!
So finance is the field that best
Accumulates his interest.
And brings him to his crowning day,
Sans pain, sans risk — and with his K!

WHAT'S IN A WORD?

In terms of etymology,
Distinguished scholars disagree
On whence the word which rules our lives —
'To Manage' — distantly derives.

But, for the 'macho' school, I fear,
One thing's indubitably clear!
The 'man' component, now as then,
Does not refer at all to 'men'!
So chauvinists invoking Adam,
Have no more claim than 'Call me madam'!

No! 'man' (your kids will understand)
Is from the latin word for 'hand';
So 'manu' would, elided, give
'By Hand' (it's in the ablative).
While 'ago' (to complete this screed)
Means 'do' 'achieve', 'perform' or 'lead'.

It doesn't matter; but I'd love
To think of 'manage' as above!
'To take by hand and lead' would seem
A more inviting kind of dream
For managers, than some whose version
Evokes the image of coercion.
Which may sound more or less absurd!
For, after all — what's in a word?